D0166941

Acclaim for *Wired and Dangerous*

"As Chip and John relay in this book, a good customer relationship is governed by honesty, caring, forgiving, lack of judgment, flexibility, and a willingness to try again. If leaders brought these values to the workplace, the world would indeed be a better place—and customers would be happier too."

—**Cheryl A. Bachelder, CEO, of AFC Enterprises Inc., and President, Popeyes Louisiana Kitchen**

"*Wired and Dangerous* is a wake-up call to business leaders about how today's empowered customers can build or destroy brands in record time. Buy it and use the insights and tools to deliver loyalty-building customer service experiences."

—**Bob Thompson, founder and CEO, CustomerThink**

"Chip and John have taught our company the power of turning satisfied customers into advocates. Their lessons in *Wired and Dangerous* lead to effective strategies for creating loyalty among today's demanding customers."

—**Carrie Freeman Parsons, Vice Chair, Freeman**

"*Wired and Dangerous* should be mandatory reading for anyone with a customer! The only downside would be a reduction in the creation of viral YouTube music videos!"

—**Dave Carroll, singer/songwriter and creator of the "United Breaks Guitars" viral YouTube music video**

"When you include your customers in your business, you build an army that grows your business for you. Using their mouse, voice, and influence, they will become your greatest megaphone! Chip and John show how the new normal customer can create the prosperity all businesses desire."

—**Jeanne Bliss, author of *Chief Customer Officer* and *I Love You More Than My Dog***

"This will be on the test: if you want customers to come and play in your backyard, read *Wired and Dangerous* and then deliver what Chip and John will teach you."

—**Jim Blasingame, host of *The Small Business Advocate Show***

"Serving customers has never been more challenging: new generations with different values, new channels, new technologies. Chip Bell and John Patterson argue that to make sense of this we need a new covenant with customers—as usual they are spot on."
—**Shaun Smith, coauthor of** *Bold*

"At Zappos, we found that the more we invested in customer service, the more loyal our customers became. *Wired and Dangerous* can help anyone interested in delivering happiness to today's Internet-empowered customer."
—**Tony Hsieh, CEO of Zappos.com, Inc., and author of the #1** *New York Times* **bestselling** *Delivering Happiness*

"Bell and Patterson explain how to master the new service paradigm—a partnership between you and your customers. Their rich stories and practical advice will prepare you to give up the control needed to make these partnership covenants succeed."
—**Charlene Li, author of** *Open Leadership* **and coauthor of the bestselling** *Groundswell*

"Provocative insight, an irresistible page-turning look at the empowered customer."
—**Lou Dobbs**

"Whether through personal anecdotes or insightful research, Chip and John have succeeded in providing the sobering truth: the consumer is more empowered than ever before and expectations for service have changed. They provide meaningful advice on how you can still succeed."
—**Jay Karen, President and CEO, Professional Association of Innkeepers International**

wired and dangerous

wired and dangerous

how your customers have changed and what to do about it

Chip R. Bell

John R. Patterson

PROPERTY OF THE LIBRARY
YORK COUNTY COMMUNITY COLLEGE
112 COLLEGE DRIVE
WELLS, MAINE 04090
(207) 646-9282

BK

Berrett–Koehler Publishers, Inc.
San Francisco
a BK Business book

The cartoon in chapter 3 used with permission from cartoonist Adrien Raeside (www.raesidecartoon.com); the cartoon in chapter 5 used with permission from the Cartoonist Group (www.cartoonistgroup.com) and cartoons in Chapters 1, 10, 11, and 12 used with permission from Cartoon Stock (www.cartoonstock.com).

Copyright © 2011 Chip R. Bell and John R. Patterson

All rights reserved. No part of this publication may be reproduced, distributed, or transmitted in any form or by any means, including photocopying, recording, or other electronic or mechanical methods, without the prior written permission of the publisher, except in the case of brief quotations embodied in critical reviews and certain other noncommercial uses permitted by copyright law. For permission requests, write to the publisher, addressed "Attention: Permissions Coordinator," at the address below.

Berrett-Koehler Publishers, Inc.
235 Montgomery Street, Suite 650
San Francisco, CA 94104-2916
Tel: (415) 288-0260   Fax: (415) 362-2512   www.bkconnection.com

Ordering Information

Quantity sales. Special discounts are available on quantity purchases by corporations, associations, and others. For details, contact the "Special Sales Department" at the Berrett-Koehler address above.

Individual sales. Berrett-Koehler publications are available through most bookstores. They can also be ordered directly from Berrett-Koehler: Tel: (800) 929-2929; Fax: (802) 864-7626; www.bkconnection.com

Orders for college textbook/course adoption use. Please contact Berrett-Koehler: Tel: (800) 929-2929; Fax: (802) 864-7626.

Orders by U.S. trade bookstores and wholesalers. Please contact Ingram Publisher Services, Tel: (800) 509-4887; Fax: (800) 838-1149; E-mail: customer.service@ingrampublisherservices.com; or visit www.ingrampublisherservices.com/Ordering for details about electronic ordering.

Berrett-Koehler and the BK logo are registered trademarks of Berrett-Koehler Publishers, Inc.

Printed in the United States of America

Berrett-Koehler books are printed on long-lasting acid-free paper. When it is available, we choose paper that has been manufactured by environmentally responsible processes. These may include using trees grown in sustainable forests, incorporating recycled paper, minimizing chlorine in bleaching, or recycling the energy produced at the paper mill.

Library of Congress Cataloging-in-Publication Data
Bell, Chip R.
  Wired and dangerous : how your customers have changed and what to do about it / Chip R. Bell, John R. Patterson.
    p. cm.
  ISBN 978-1-60509-975-0 (pbk. : alk. paper)
  1. Customer relations.   2. Customer services.   3. Customer loyalty.   4. Internet.
I. Patterson, John R. (John Rice), 1951–   II. Title.
  HF5415.5.B43835 2011
  658.8'12—dc22
                                        2011009393

Cover Designer: Susan Malikowski, DesignLeaf Studio
Text designer: Adriane Bosworth
Proofreader: Katherine Lee
Indexer: Kirsten Kite
Book producer: Detta Penna

Contents

PART THREE

Suggestions for Partnering with Customers

Flash Drive: Tools and Favorites 165

Tools

Favorites

Notes   223

Bibliography   233

Thanks   236

Index   239

About the Authors   247

PART ONE

The Situation
Welcome to Turbulent Times!

> It was the best of times, it was the worst of times, . . .
> it was the season of Light, it was the season of Dark-
> ness, it was the spring of hope, it was the winter of
> despair, we had everything before us, we had nothing
> before us.
>
> Charles Dickens
A Tale of Two Cities

These words opened Charles Dickens's classic book *A Tale of Two Cities,* written 150 years ago. The passage was Dickens's elegant attempt to describe the late 1700s as the bridge between two eras; the era of the farm was transitioning to the era of the factory. That transition saw great upheaval, including several major revolutionary wars; it was also a period of extensive invention and discovery. If Dickens were here today he might use similar words to describe the present time—as a bridge between the period of technology and the era of the customer.

Whether or not you accept the hyperbole of an emerging revolution, there is no doubt customers today are significantly different than those of just a few years ago. Then, we were easily wooed by the new restaurant with the cool sign or catchy brand name. Then, a call center that quickly answered the phone got high marks, even if the rep had an attitude, or simply couldn't answer our question and transferred us from Patty to Paul to pillar to post. Then, we excused indifferent service on the grounds that someone was having a bad day, but gave little thought to voicing our displeasure or abandoning the service provider.

Who was then best known for excellent service? Nordstrom! The upscale department store was staffed by friendly people willing, for instance, to accompany us to other departments in the store, and in all ways to provide customized service—something practically every gas station attendant on the planet did for our grandparents. At that time, service had to be really awful for us to walk away. Brands were important to us and we stuck with them for a lifetime. Our fathers bought the same brand of automobile every three years for their entire lives.

Those days are completely gone. Welcome to the turbulent times of the "new normal" customer—restless, cautious, powerful, and potentially dangerous.

The Rise of the New Normal

The landscape of customer service has been re-contoured. Today's customers are not at all the way they used to be 20 years ago. What has caused customers to be so different today? First, customers get terrific service from some organizations and use those experiences to judge everyone else. When the UPS or FedEx delivery person walks to our front door with a sense of urgency, we expect the mail carrier to do likewise. When the Disney associate treats us as a special guest, we assume every other frontline service person will be as friendly. We look at every e-tailer through Amazon.com and Zappos.com eyes. We compare every great service experience to every other service experience.

Customers also have far more choices than ever before. Go to the grocery store for a loaf of bread and you are confronted with 16 brands and 23 varieties packaged 12 different ways. Three decades ago sliced bread came one way—white—and was probably produced by either

Wonder or Sunbeam. Today, product choices proliferate and have fewer apparent differences, so customers are forced to use the quality of their purchase experience surrounding the product as their primary means for discernment and decision making. How much is Hertz really different from Avis or Budget? Marriott from Hyatt or Hilton? FedEx from UPS? Today's customers are much smarter buyers than their parents were. The Internet has become a potent source of real-time education. According to research reported by *New York Times* Pulitzer Prize–winning reporter Matt Richtel, people consume an average of 12 hours of media a day (when an hour spent with the Internet and TV simultaneously counts as two hours). That compares with five hours in 1960.[1]

The Internet is a tool for instant assessment. Considering Sleepwell Hotel for your next vacation trip? You can instantly get web-based information complete with evaluations from forty-eleven previous guests. We are our own *Consumer Reports*. Watchdog websites can give you the lowdown on why Joe's Pretty Good Car Repair is better than Otto's Auto.

Recent data from Society for New Communications Research shows that 84 percent of customers consider the quality of a provider's customer service when deciding whether to do business with the company.[2] This means companies must monitor all the details of their customer service—now very transparent to customers—and provide super-early warning on emerging glitches. It means creating customer conversations that promote insight and foster trust. It also means never forgetting that, armed with deep knowledge from a myriad of sources, customers are more empowered and emboldened to "balk and walk." The organization that hangs their reputation on a solid brand or on the reach and influence of carefully crafted PR is, as they say in the South where we live, "just asking for a whuppin'!"

A merchant of yesteryear, placed on truth serum, might have described customers as a bit gullible, very nice, conflict-averse, easily influenced by advertising, not particularly savvy, and willing to accept average quality. No more. Today's labels would not be so meek and mild. In fact, a contemporary merchant would no doubt acknowledge the power and influence customers now wield.

Today, the customer really is king. Enabled and equipped by the Internet, with its capacity to instantly reach a gazillion fellow customers with the click of a mouse, customers can bring any service provider to its knees. The new normal customer, with this newfound strength, is no more the small and subservient victim of the stereotypically colossal and greedy corporation of yesteryear. The tables of the customer relationship have been turned. Plentiful product and service information has created a more mature customer. Customers today are wired and dangerous.

Turning Back the Covers

The French Revolution was triggered by a series of events that led to the storming of the Bastille to release long-held political prisoners. Only the common people were paying taxes; nobles and clergy were exempt. The price of France's participation in the American Revolution had taken a heavy financial toll. Then, King Louis XVI helped bankrupt the French government by spending lavishly on his court at Versailles. In response, the French government attempted to squeeze even more revenue from already cash-strapped citizens.

Meanwhile, the writings of Enlightenment thinkers like Voltaire and Rousseau, which focused on the worth of all people, were gaining popularity. As French soldiers who fought in the American Revolution returned to France, they brought with them incendiary stories of the fight for liberty and equality. These smoldering ideas required little more to spark revolt. When Queen Marie Antoinette was told that the common people were without bread, she supposedly remarked "Let them eat cake!" Rumor of her haughty insensitivity spread through the streets, inciting even peace-loving citizens to take up arms.

What does this French history lesson tell us? For anyone with a customer: signs of change can emerge unexpectedly. Alarm bells are ringing for us. Customers who have more choices and more smarts, and who have experienced great service from some, now expect the same standards from everyone. The bar has been raised.

As with the French Revolution, the root causes of our changing consumer expectations have existed for a long time. Responding to the superficial signs of change can be tactically helpful. It is what most organizations have done. But, addressing what is underneath is the secret strategy that will spark continuing customer loyalty in this new business environment. It is the path to increased profits and growth.

The Guitar Heard Around the World

After musician Dave Carroll learned from fellow passengers that United Airlines baggage handlers were damaging his guitar on the Chicago O'Hare tarmac, he was unable to find anyone at United willing to make the situation right, so he made a music video about his woes. He posted the video on YouTube, chronicling in humorous detail United's failure to provide appropriate service and their limp approach to repairing or reconciling the situation. This negative view of the United brand has been viewed by well over 9 million people! The juicy cyber battle has been cited endlessly as an example of what not to do both in the media and in print. According to a blog written by *The Economist* and posted on July 24, 2009, the Dave Carroll incident cost United Airlines 10 percent of share value, or about $180 million![3]

The impact on United is not surprising in a world where, according to recent Convergys research, *social media has five times the impact of traditional word of mouth*. Think of social media as word of mouth on steroids. The average post is read by 45 people, and 62 percent of customers who hear about a bad experience on social media stop doing business with, or avoid doing business with, the offending company.[4]

Only a few years ago Dave would have had to work his way through the United bureaucracy, and would most likely only have been able to spread the word of his frustration by telling his story to friends and family members. Perhaps he would have found a "consumer advocate" willing to tell his story on radio or television, which may have brought enough leverage to goad United into action. Not today! Dave rebelled and brought his story graphically in a music video to the power of the Internet and word of his situation spread at warp speed.

Now, for the really scary part. Although Dave's damaged-guitar troubles happened in the spring of 2008 and his first video went on YouTube in July 2009, his video continues to harm the United brand as it hangs around cyberspace. Unlike word of mouth, which fades as other events crowd it out of memory, word of *mouse* missives remain out there like a tribal story repeated down the generations.

Attacks on a brand through customer blogs, Yelp-like reviews, social media, and YouTube-like messages dangerous to a brand cannot be cured by a booster shot of good will. They become a chronic disease that weakens a reputation, even if they are without merit. If United Airlines had quickly apologized and involved Dave in crafting the best restitution (maybe two first-class tickets to Disney World plus repairing or replacing his Taylor guitar), and communicated the changes implemented based on their learnings, the Internet pedestrian might have never known about the United fiasco. United's experience with Dave Carroll suggests the wisdom of nipping in the bud anything that could rapidly become a PR nightmare.

Technology has made today's customers powerful and potentially dangerous. While CEOs and CFOs focus on stock prices and raising capital, customers zero in on getting fair value—and that now includes a positive service experience. Today's customers have the capacity to bring down popular brands, squeeze corporate balance sheets, and send stock prices plummeting.

Rethinking Service

Once upon a time, captains of industry worried about the fallout from failed *products* (Ford Explorer, Tylenol, Toyota); now they must worry about the downside of failed *service* (JetBlue, AOL, United). The implications of failed service present a much bigger challenge. Think about it this way: organizations determine the quality of the products they put out in the marketplace, but *customers* determine the lion's share of whether their *service* has quality. Riding herd on what happens in the factory is a lot more predictable and controllable than getting customers to do what is expected on their side of the service equation.

Industry captains who have been surprised by the tone, mindset, and muscle of today's customers are misunderstanding the real meaning of service. Using product thinking, with its emphasis on quality control and backroom domination, they put the spotlight on the service outcome—not on the service *experience*. "What do you mean, customers are upset by their banking experience? Our statements are accurate and our tellers are efficient!" "How could passengers be upset? We got them to their destination safely, on time, and with their luggage!" They see a good outcome but are not assessing the customer experience. Both outcome and experience are important to the customer. But often the outcome is, to the customer, simply a table stake—the givens of the service provided and not what distinguishes it.

McDonald's is an excellent hamburger factory, one of the best in the world. McDonald's CEO can no doubt tell you the average speed of service per car at 12:32 p.m., the precise amount of time required to make a Big Mac, the pace of a credit-card transaction versus cash— essentially, the arithmetic of the service encounter. These are all metrics almost completely controllable by McDonald's. But the customer is evaluating their trip to Mickey D's based on the personality of the server, the hospitality of the setting, and the respect they are shown throughout the entire process. These are metrics co-created by McDonald's and the customer. McDonald's controls their presentation, but the customer determines if the entire experience made the grade.

When organizations rely on professional shoppers to assess the experience of the customer rather than asking the customer directly, they reveal their product-making mentality. Shoppers are actors trained to watch for adherence to standards, much like the quality-control department does in a factory. Real customers have a broader view, a memory-making perspective that considers both outcome and experience.

John has five children. Ask John's wife what is more important:

the speed with which the order was filled, the expected level of food preparation, or the welcoming attitude of the server. She will tell you that style is more important than speed in determining whether she returns! Sure, the basic outcome expectation is for fast food *fast*, but the experience is what is remembered. Call centers the world over, whether B2C or B2B, stay up late worrying about speed of answer and call handle time (outcome metrics), forgetting customer research shows that first-call resolution and knowledgeability of the call center rep are more important to customers (experience measures).[5]

The edginess of today's powerful wired and dangerous customers has been fueled by more than just a change in their service expectations. The energy behind their newfound assertiveness is a fundamental change in what we call the *service covenant*—the unspoken people-serving-people contract that has been the essence of commerce for centuries. When service providers completely remove the high touch from their high tech service without the consent, consideration, or participation of the customer, they erode customer confidence, create suspicion, and trigger impulses often expressed as thoughts of an "I'm outa here" mutiny.

Wired and Dangerous: What Lies Ahead (Please Read This Part!)

Wired and Dangerous is first and foremost a picture of today's new normal customer. We refer to customers as wired and dangerous because they are edgy as well as connected with the Internet-enabled capacity to rapidly gain insight on a particular product or service and to quickly do great harm to the reputation of service providers.

That's not to say that all customers are technologically wired. Neither of our 86- and 94-year-old mothers is computer savvy—but they are still wired and potentially dangerous. How's that? Our mothers are personally connected with many who *are* wired. An unpleasant experience at the grocery store can trigger a disparaging comment to a neighbor who has a social network and a proclivity for pinging Internet-savvy friends. Overnight, a casual comment like "Their meat made me kinda sick" can trigger a social media–driven boycott that makes a sizable dent in the grocery store's profits. So, even the technologically unskilled customer is dangerous.

More than sounding a warning for all who serve customers, this book provides a compelling rationale for today's customer restlessness and gives concrete solutions for turning customer admonition into approval and annoyance into advocacy. We have laced the book with an array of highly practical, put-in-place-today suggestions. You will find relevant best-practice examples and heart-tugging stories about those who got it right and some who missed. While the book is intended to stimulate insights and *aha*'s, it is also a pragmatic recipe for delivering better service while improving long-term relationships with customers.

We will say this later in more elegant ways: we love customers. We truly believe most customers are without malice and possess a keen sense of fairness. We are major fans of customer loyalty—even devotion. Our consulting work with clients is focused on one objective: to help them find ways to increase customer loyalty. Our labels in the book are designed to be descriptive, not judgmental or pejorative. However, the conditions adversely impacting what we will later describe as the age-old service covenant have created in far too many customers a sense of mistrust, disappointment and, given the right circumstances, even anger. Our intent in writing this book is to encourage the righting of a service covenant that has been flipped over and to facilitate moving customer relationships from skeptical indifference to wholesome partnerships.

This book is not exclusively about the online customer. Forrester Research projected e-commerce sales in the United States will grow at a 10 percent compound annual growth rate through 2014. E-commerce sales will represent 8 percent of all retail sales in the U.S. by 2014, up from 6 percent in 2009. Forrester also estimates that online and web-influenced offline sales combined accounted for 42 percent of total retail sales in 2009, and projects that percentage to grow to 53 percent by 2014. The bottom line is this: despite the dramatic influence of the Internet, customers are still going to a store to make most of their purchases.[6] But more and more they are going to the store educated and influenced by what they learned online.

Readers sometimes are curious about the logic of a book cover. We hope most will be obvious. The cover of the book is a metaphor for what we portend in the expression "wired and dangerous." We selected black with caution-light yellow to convey a sense of warning. We made the title and subtitle all lower case to reinforce the idea that the Internet has enabled a disgruntled customer disposition to become dangerous because of its speed and reach. "Customers on fire" have always been a challenge to service providers. But, "customers on fire online" have exponentially increased that threat. The "Wi-Fi" symbol continues the cyber-theme started by lower case, Internet-looking fonts. Finally, we chose the book endorsement by Zappos.com CEO and Founder Tony Hsieh because we believe his Internet-based company and the principles that have guided its amazing success reflect a practical application of the philosophy of *Wired and Dangerous.*

The book is organized into three parts. Part One (Chapters 1 to 5) describes the situation, Part Two (Chapters 6 to 12) outlines the solutions, and Part Three—we call this section "Flash Drive"— contains tools for implementing the solutions. Don't look for a ton of how-to's in the first part. We thought it was important to first provide a comprehensive understanding of today's customers before launching into the approaches needed to correct problems, close gaps, and repair broken components. We think we more than made up for the dearth of how-to's in Part One with the generous helping in Parts Two and Three. As a reminder, we have included occasional "go to" sidebars with suggestions of specific tools related to the content nearby.

The text also includes what we call "e-sights," brief inserts designed to be food for thought. Think of them as insights for the cyber age! For our many readers who like any anecdotal presentation to be backed up by concrete, scientific evidence, we have included a bounty of solid, contemporary customer research. We provide more than a hundred citations plus a detailed bibliography for those wanting to pursue topics in more detail.

Our target reader for this book is everyone who directly serves a customer or who supports someone who serves a customer. As we wrote *Wired and Dangerous*, we envisioned readers in small enterprises as well as in very large companies. We assumed our audience to be front-line employees as well as executives. For readers in leadership roles, we included a special tool in the Flash Drive part specifically written for you.

We viewed our audience as employees in for-profit, not-for-profit, and governmental organizations as well as mom-and-pop enterprises and sole proprietorships. We crafted the book for organizations that serve customers (B2C) as well as businesses that service other businesses (B2B). At the end of the day, all organizations have customers and all customers are people. Even the most business-to-business (B2B) company is really people-to-people (P2P).

To learn and gain the most from *Wired and Dangerous*, it might help to remember the adage "We are all self-employed." Even if you are not in an influential change agent role or the senior leader at the top of the organizational food chain, unless you are in solitary confinement you have some control over ways to enhance the experience of your customers (or those you serve). With a clear picture of the work you would like to do, coupled with a bit of courage, you can always help even the most inwardly focused, rule-entrenched, customer-hostile company move a step closer to being a partner with customers and creating experiences that are positively memorable. At the very least, you are in complete control of your own attitude and the passion you transmit to those you serve.

Don't think that what is today will also be tomorrow. The future will be even more challenging! However, we believe the path ahead contains great hope, clear opportunity, and fruitful adventure. Think of this book as your periscope to the future and a guide to ready you for the trip. This is a working book—one aimed at being more edgy than conventional, more vivacious than staid, more sensible than scholarly—and much more about practice than philosophy. We hope you enjoy the trip and that you'll let us know what you think of it. The last page of the book contains ways to reach us easily. We invite you to join our blogs and tweets. Let's have a conversation about serving today's wired and dangerous customers.

/\/\/\\/

Customers with a beef or a boast have always been able to share it with their friends. The difference today is that the reach of their connection via the Internet is enormous; the speed of their link is instantaneous. Imagine how quickly the peasants of France could have organized the French Revolution had all of them had a Facebook, Foursquare, or LinkedIn account! Or, if the French writers of messages of resistance had been able to blog their dissent for all to read in real time, thus to coordinate a flash demonstration, boycott, or protest. Wired to an army of like-minded people looking for answers, today's customers can be dangerous to any service provider unwilling to understand what customers want, adapt to the way they want it, and deliver what they find of value.

"Revolution is not the uprising against preexisting order," wrote Spanish philosopher José Ortega y Gasset, "but the setting up of a new order contradictory to the traditional one." Out of turbulent economic times comes a new order. According to recent research by American Express, 9 in 10 Americans (91 percent) consider the level of customer service important when deciding to do business with a company. But only 24 percent of Americans believe companies value their business and will go the extra mile to keep it.[7] A 2010 report from RightNow and Harris Interactive indicates that 82 percent of consumers in the United States said they've *stopped* doing business with a company due to a poor customer service experience. Ninety-five percent of customers said after a bad customer experience they would "take action." [8]

Those who fail will be those brought down by failing to modify their patterns and practices. Those who succeed will be the ones who embrace the opportunity by shifting their outlook and their operation. They want to repair and maintain the service covenant through a true partnership—an alliance that respects the needs of all and values the pursuit of continuing growth and unending elasticity. [9]

CHAPTER 1

How the Service Covenant Became Corrupted

The service covenant has been around for centuries. It is grounded in the concept of the direct or implied pledge of fair bartering—a merchant provides a product or service in exchange for some type of remuneration. Energy might be spent on either side of the covenant as to the fairness of the exchange (server spending energy on promotion; customer spending energy on getting perceived worth), but the essence of the agreement remained intact. There was a promise implied on both sides of the encounter

The covenant for a *product* was different from the covenant for a service. Customers gave the product provider license to make the product without their participation, or even observation. You did not need to watch the maker of your basket or your dishwasher; you could trust it would be as promised. The tangible nature of an object made the determination of quality easier. As customers, we expected the product would be as described and we had recourse if it was not—typically the object could be returned for a replacement or our coconuts or coins would be returned if it failed to meet the value we were promised. Replacement meant another object like the one we purchased was taken from inventory and given to us. In this fashion the covenant could be restored. [1]

The *service* covenant has some similarities. There were expectations of features and benefits, as for a product. Energy around

> Your call is important to us, just not as important as whatever else we're doing.

Streeter

promotion and price was also similar. However, since service was large-ly experiential, it could not be stockpiled, inventoried, or sent back for a replacement. Consequently, recourse for a broken promise could not be in kind. Displeasure with your haircut might get you a discount on your next one but there was no way to get your hair back like it was.

So, what was the recourse hardwired into the service covenant? The customer derived some comfort or security through the fact that service would be delivered through an experience which the customer co-created with the service provider. The inclusion of nods, clicks, sounds, and sighs both from customer and service provider during the co-creation process provided customers a way to be the guardian of their side of the transaction. As a haircut customer you could say "Not so much on the sides!" early enough in the experience to prevent the outcome from being a disappointment you were then forced to wear.

Unlike a product, a service is produced at the moment of delivery. You cannot create it in advance. You cannot send the customer a sample to be inspected and approved. Unlike a product, the receiver of a service gets nothing tangible, and value depends on the receiver's experience and perception. As the service provider, you might be able to plan presentation, people-manners, and processes, but for almost all services it was not deemed a "service received" until it was experienced by (or with) the customer.

Should a product provider opt to change the way the product was manufactured or redo the manner that inventory was organized, it could all be accomplished with minimal impact on (or involvement from) the customer. However, alter the way the service experience occurs and the covenant is fundamentally changed.

Let's examine a metaphor. When banks got the bright idea of using ATMs instead of a teller, they encountered sizable resistance. ATM use was less than 15 percent even ten years after the machines were introduced. Compare that to the speed of adoption of smart phones or Netflix. The ATM fundamentally altered the nature of the service experience. Now, don't push this ATM metaphor too far by examining it in light of today's use. We all know customers today enjoy the convenience of the ATM plus the warmth of dialogue with Peggy. ATM acceptance changed when tellers stood outside the bank and taught customers how to use them, allaying fears about the security of a deposit placed in an uncaring, automated machine.

Progress requires change, and change provokes resistance. However, customers do not necessarily resist change itself. They resist the perception or prediction of being controlled or coerced without their involvement. They accept change when they get a vote; they embrace change when they can participate.

> **E-SIGHT**
>
> The remedy for buying a faulty product that disappointed was getting to return or exchange it. The recourse for buying a faulty service was getting to stop it, influence it, or change it in the middle of the experience. Giving the service experience the features of a product is like putting lipstick on a pig. It may make the pig look better, but it doesn't make 'em happy.

Alteration in the service covenant has been fueled by the push for cost cutting and efficiency. Migrating customers toward self-service, for example, brings an array of time-saving benefits to both service provider and service receiver. But the manner in which that migration typically occurs—without influence from customers—can be viewed as devaluing the co-creator, thus adding another spark to the flame of their opposition.

The Rebellious Customer

Customers today are picky, fickle, vocal, and vain.[2] They are *picky* in that they are more cautious in their choices (and they have many more choices) than customers of yesteryear and are interested only in getting obvious value for their money. They are more informed about the choices available, smarter in choice-making, and more selective in whom they elect to join. They are *fickle* in that they are much quicker to leave if unhappy. They show a lower tolerance for error, and will exit even when the service is merely indifferent.

Customers today are *vocal* in that they are both quick and loud in registering concerns based on their higher standards for value and their expectation of getting a tailored response. They assertively tell others their views of an organization's service; they also pay attention to fellow customers' negative reviews and make choices without even giving the organization a chance. A 2009 Nielsen online survey of 25,000 consumers in more than fifty countries found that customers trusted friends, family, and peers for product recommendations 90 percent of the time.[3] Finally, they are *vain* in that they expect treatment that telegraphs they are special and unique.

Now we know, as customers ourselves, that the picky, fickle and vocal parts are spot on. The vain label may seem harsh. Few of us look in the mirror and see a vain person looking back. But, the "Have it your way!" perspective we have acquired is the natural byproduct of pampering by service providers. Customer self-centeredness has been enlarged by our newfound muscle in the marketplace. Be honest. How would you react if you bought a product that turned out to be defective and the merchant refused to take it back? What if the McDonald's counter clerk told you they would not "hold the cheese" on your Big Mac? We *enjoy* some degree of service personalization; we also expect it!

The picky-fickle-vocal-vain moniker represents a dramatic shift as we look at what is required to ensure customer loyalty—the stuff of growth and profits. Customer requirements for value are way out of sync with the tried and true methods organizations have relied on for years. When frontline employees deliver service that fulfils the customer's stated needs, they are taken aback when customers give them less than satisfactory grades. When a small gaffe triggers volcano-like customer uproar, many frontline employees believe they have met a deranged deviant with an attitude problem, not just a typical customer acting on instincts honed from countless disappointments.

The more dissonance there is between what the server provides and the served receives, the more the problem exacerbates. Customers declare the organization's frontline ambassadors are indifferent, difficult, and uncaring. Further, the connections customers now have with one another via the Internet and social media give them the power to transform an organization overnight from service *champ* to service *chump*. Customers formerly loyal to a particular brand now regard brand identification as just PR drivel or corporate snake oil. Add to this cacophony a global playing field, razor-thin margins, warp-speed change, and depleted staffing levels, and you have a recipe for employee *wear-out* and customer *walk-out*.

It is not that organizations are responding less but that they are responding incorrectly—out of sync with what new customers require.

They are "efforting" but not achieving. Those who recast their engagement strategy in innovative ways are resonating with the "new" customers and winning their loyalty.

Take a look at award-winning Zappos.com, now a part of Amazon.com. They took a simple business—online buying of shoes—and added the experience enhancers that make them the talk of the neighborhood (and cyberhood). Sure, you can do all your buying without communicating with a soul. But, every Zappos web page has a deliberate invitation to interact. When the customer clicks to talk, they get over-the-top attention, customized communication, and a live rep who wants to be your new best friend. Zappos merchandise arrives at your front door way before you have a chance to wonder when it will. It is the perfect blend of self-service with full service that respects the service covenant while bolstering convenience and cost savings. And, how has the market rewarded them? Their profits went from zero when they started to over $1 billion 10 years later.

Customers are primed and ready for uprising. Some have already jumped ship to pursue a new service provider that offers greater value. Under the surface of picky-fickle-vocal-vain is a level of frustration (sometimes anger) that is fueling their mutinous and sometimes dangerous behavior. This book is about the tainted groundwater of customer discontent—and how to fix it. Addressing the symptoms while ignoring the cause is like taking an aspirin for bronchitis—it may make you feel better temporarily, but failing to address the real issue can lead to customer churn and, more devastatingly, a customer-led uprising trafficked on the Internet. Turning a potentially dangerous customer into an advocate is not only possible but it is also eagerly desired by those you serve.

The Museum of Customer Service

A stroll through a museum filled with artifacts of an earlier time can be enlightening; that trip down memory lane can teach us a lot about where we were. In the words of George Santayana, "Those who do not learn from history are doomed to repeat it."[4] The museum shows us how we have changed.

Pretend there was a Museum of Customer Service. You would see objects of the past, like fax machines and floppy disks. You would see hotels with phones in guest rooms that guests actually used for more than a request for a wake-up call. In the museum, plumbers cost less than dentists; all banks were open until noon on Saturday. Retail stores had sales clerks on the floor, not just at the register. Grocery stores had bakers, gas stations had a mechanic, and mail-order catalogues were all-purpose, not just specialty. Stores had layaway plans and returns clerks; banks had signature loans. Doctors made house calls and treated whatever malady they encountered, rarely referring the patient to anyone else.

Looking forward from the past, what has changed? The most obvious change has been a dramatic trend toward self-service. We skip the check-out counter with the long line and moving-in-slow-motion cashier to do self-checkout. We let our fingers do the walking, not in the antiquated phone book but through search engines like Google, Bing, and Yahoo, for what we want to buy. We look at Overstock and eBay for bargains, YouTube for entertainment, Wikipedia for reference, and Mapquest for directions. Buying online has altered the service experience as dramatically as the disappearance of the friendly elevator operator who could tell you that Housewares is on the third floor.

Self-service has had a positive side. Shifting the lion's share of the service experience to the customer has lowered operating costs. It has freed up human resources to be used in roles and functions truly requiring a human touch. Self-service has also made the customer more self-reliant, as "do-it-yourself" has replaced "I'll take care of that for you." Learning to fend for oneself can trigger acquisition of both knowledge and confidence. Customers are less dependent and far more competent.

Let's go back to our French history lesson for a minute. In 1789, reading Voltaire or hearing tales of freedom from French soldiers just back from the American Revolution were both double-edged swords.

French commoners were inspired, but they were also emboldened. Similarly today, self-service is a tool for independence that has a "revolutionary" or dark side as well. That under-the-surface component, properly managed, can be an opportunity for service greatness leading to customer growth and bottom line profits.

Service is the act of giving assistance to a customer. When most of the "assisting" is shifted to the recipient by the provider, resentment often ensues: "Why am I having to do this myself?" As customers, we ultimately get over it, learning to pump our own gas, find our own size, and wash our own cars. We stop using tellers and librarians and go straight to a machine. But with the change of balance between serving and being served comes an alteration in the true meaning of service. Many years ago, if the elevator operator was out on break, we felt underserved. Today, an elevator is not even viewed as a context for service, it is just a functional device to move us up and down.

Self-service changes our standards for service. Obviously, when we "do it our way" we get highly tailor-made service. As customers, this changes how we view those who serve us. We assume they will know us almost as well as we know ourselves. We think they can read our minds. We assume that getting us what we want, the way we want it, will be as big a deal to them as it is to us.

Looking forward from the Museum of Customer Service also reveals a migration toward service isolation. There was a time when a call to a business yielded a switchboard operator on the other end who sent our call to just the right person. Not only did operators sound like neighbors but they also knew who in the organization did what. Today, an IVR (interactive voice response) computer screens the call. Insist on speaking to a live person and you are likely to get an operator in Mumbai or Singapore—someone who probably does not sound like a neighbor. The 2010 Contact Center Satisfaction Index (CCSI) from the CFI Group found that offshore contact centers scored 27 percent lower in customer satisfaction than those based in the United States.[5]

As social animals, we enjoy the experiential and interpersonal side of service. Removing the "assistant" leaves us going it alone. We rely on customer reviews since there is no helpful clerk to tell us the features we might have missed. We order online in silence without benefit of banter with the service provider. While the time-saving, service-at-any-hour components are very appealing, in our hearts we sometimes wish for more of a connection, even at the expense of less convenience.

A front page *USA Today* article highlighted the return of travel customers to travel agents from online travel sites. Quoted in the article, travel agent Suzanne Burr said, "Customers would push the button on some of these websites, and that was it. There was nobody to ask a question. Nobody to ask for help. When it comes to really spending money and wanting an advocate, people are turning back to agents because people care. A computer doesn't." To confirm the point, a study by Forrester Research found that, in the first three months of 2010, 28 percent of leisure travelers in the United States who booked their trips online said they'd be interested in going to a traditional travel agent.[6]

The Museum of Customer Service also reveals that there has been a swing toward a reliance on experts or specialists. We often hear "We don't carry that item, check with . . ." or "I need to refer you to . . . " or, the unkindest cut of all, "You might look it up online." The "all-purpose" has been stripped out of most service encounters. Where did you buy your last TV—at Sears or at Best Buy? How about the last book you bought—did you check out the book section of Wal-Mart, or go to a Borders bookstore, or log on to Amazon.com? We go for fishing gear at Bubba's Bait Shop only for convenience. Otherwise, it's Bass ProShops, Cabela's, or—again—online. Most of our clothing comes from stores that sell only clothing, not from a J.C. Penney. Need a new bicycle? The specialist at the bike shop down the street probably takes care of the cyclists en route to the next triathlon.

So, there are mixed blessings. With specialists comes expertise not found in the generic service encounter. Service providers with unique competence give us confidence in our purchase or experience. Good ones mentor us, leaving us smarter than we were before; poor ones anger us with their arrogance and "hide the ball" tactics. With specialists comes the proliferation of "silos," organizational turf boundaries put in place for the convenience of those who "manage" processes that supposedly serve the customer. In reality, these artificial boundaries can make the customer's experience much more challenging.

John recently tried to refinance a home-equity line with a large bank where he has been a customer for thirty years. His loyalty to the provider mattered not! He was repeatedly subjected to the dreaded "That is not my department, you will need to call another 800 number," making the process frustrating and cumbersome. All in the name of speaking with experts. Guess what John did? He went to a smaller bank that maintains the service covenant the old-fashioned way— face-to-face conversation with bankers who work to build a relationship, not service a transaction.

Chip recently purchased a television, sound bar, and receiver from Best Buy for his rather remote second home. Connecting the TV to the receiver was easy. However, connecting the sound bar to the receiver was not. Nothing in the three manuals covered the unique connection (sound bars typically are plugged directly into the TV, not a receiver). When he called Best Buy to ask "Into which receiver hole do I plug the sound bar cord?" he was transferred to tech support. Ready to explain his situation and get a quick answer, he was instead told that a technology professional would have to come to his house and show him where to plug in the cord—at a fee of $150. He had just spent $1,500! When he then tried to schedule an onsite visit by Best Buy's notorious Geek Squad, after a 90-minute phone call he was finally told he was outside their service range. What would Sears have done, ten or fifteen years ago?

One annoyance that comes with relying on the expertise of specialists is the search for the right one. Being dependent on experts also undermines the classless nature of being served by someone "like us," who has only slightly more knowledge than we have. Being served by a generalist was rather neighborly and egalitarian. There is now a potentially uncomfortable distance between customer and specialist. We sometimes miss the bond and wish for a richer relationship, not just a smarter one. We want to be a partner, not a patient!

Constantly dealing with experts has already altered our standards for the service provided by non-experts. Customers assume the competence of every expert and assume expertise in every service provider. Will customers now expect all frontline employees to be the smartest, best resourced, most empowered service providers imaginable?

The shift toward self-service with reliance on experts has taken the *conversation* out of service. Social media is filling the void. The twenty-something customer, skilled at text messaging, views a phone call as an interruption. For the teenager, being able to communicate "PAW" (parents are watching) to a friend via text, or just code number 9, keeps the cyberlog intimate. Yet the removal of all non-verbals (body language, facial expressions) from the conversation increases the risk of misunderstanding.

The foundation for great service is grounded not in the superficial tenets of contemporary service but in the core of the human condition when partnering is present. Even as customers enjoy the blessings of high-tech service, they want a high-*touch* partner when they need help. Partnerships with customers work if they are participative, egalitarian connections rich with compassion and humanity, filled with the collective capacity to personalize, and inspired by the nobility of giving assistance to another. The profits of companies like Amazon.com, Netflix, Zappos.com—companies that work to blend high tech with high touch—provide evidence that a partnership philosophy pays off.

/\/\/\/

Voltaire, a popular writer during the era of the French Revolution, was as prophetic as he was poetic. His line "Better is the enemy of good" has been oft quoted (and misquoted) but stands as one of the tenets of remarkable service.[7] He also wrote (without realizing it) about the antidote to the woes of current customer service: "We are rarely proud when we are alone."[8] Viewing service as an economic watering hole is a critical path to remarkable service.

CHAPTER 2

Picky

Why Today's Customers Are Finicky

> Customers today want the very most and the very
> best for the very least amount of money, and on the
> best terms.
>
> Brian Tracy
> *Now, Build a Great Business*

Chip recently fired his insurance agent—and hired a new one! "The old insurance agent did absolutely nothing bad," Chip said, "and the office clerk was always friendly when I called."

It's just that the agent never did anything other than write my insurance policies and send me annual bills. The agent never called to thank me for my business, opting instead for a form letter only at renewal time. And, this is a small insurance office in a small town, not some mega-business with a gazillion customers!

The straw that broke the camel's back was when I called one Wednesday afternoon just minutes past noon to inquire about getting a new umbrella policy. I heard a recording stating that the agency office always closed at noon on Wednesday but would reopen at 9 o'clock on Thursday morning. There was no answering service to channel my call should this have been an insurance emergency. So, I considered sending an email. I Googled the agency name only to find they had no website; there was no email address on any of their correspondence. If this were 1950, such practices might have made more sense.

Chip's new insurance agent (from the same insurance carrier, mind you) is always available. In the first phone call the new agent took a quick look at Chip's five policies—home, two cars, a boat, and a valuables policy—and informed him that the homeowners policy he had was outdated and a newer one could provide better features and reduce his premium 40 percent. He also indicated that Chip's boat policy was based on the purchase price and the boat's value had depreciated by 30 percent, dictating lower coverage and a lower premium. Then, the agent backed up his words with a detailed email. Chip's "terminated" agent had never bothered to shift him to these better offerings.

Today's customers have learned from situations like Chip's to be picky. Not only do they expect value for their hard-earned, ever-challenged income, they absolutely demand it. That value not only applies to product but it also applies to their experience. Remember, their experience yardstick is developed from the remarkable interactions with service providers that occur in all aspects of their life. Chip wasn't measuring his former insurance provider only against other insurance providers. He was measuring that experience against all of the great experiences across all aspects of his life, and obviously the service the former agent provided fell way short! Customers' standards for value have been raised to a level that makes average, okay service deemed less than valuable. Chip's close encounter with service mediocrity was enough to trigger a divorce; it was not a service hiccup that ended the relationship, just the realization that improvement in value was not in the offing.

Picky Proof

You might think the shift to focusing on customer experience would trigger an emphasis on getting better. But customers say that they have not seen a focus on improvement. In a recent survey of several thousand customers in a variety of industries, over three-fourths of respondents indicated the quality of customer service provided had either stayed the same or gotten worse.[1] And, what do employees and executives think? Fifty percent of them thought service had improved.[2] Perhaps it had. But, the expectations of customers have climbed even faster. You may say your service grade has gone from a C+ to a B. But, to the customer, yesterday's B is today's C.

VALUE RULES!

2010 customers were 39 percent more likely to select "a good value for the money" as the top attribute than 2009 customers.

Convergys
2010 Scorecard Research

Convergys is favorite customer research firm. Annually, they conduct a survey of thousands of customers, frontline employees, and executives in search of what matters most to customers. Their target sample of customers is chosen from nine key industries ranging from telecommunications to retail to financial services. Their cutting-edge research often runs counter to conventional wisdom, causing service providers to rethink their approach to creating customer experiences that build loyalty.

According to Convergys research, 45 percent of customers think companies do not understand what their customers really experience when dealing with them. Yet, 80 percent of employees and executives think they understand. This could suggest that more leaders take turns on the front line—ear to ear and face to face with customers. Finally, 39 percent of customers think that companies do not listen to or act on customer feedback; yet (and here's the largest gap between the customer's view and the company's perception) 87 percent of employees and executives believe "we listen."[3]

All of this comes at a time when customer expectations are rising. Recent research by Accenture showed customer expectations were 33 percent higher than the year before.[4] According to the Society for New

Communications Research, rather than rely on a trusted brand, 74 percent of customers choose some providers based on other customers' service experience and 84 percent consider a provider's customer-care quality when deciding whether to do business with a company.[5]

Just as many of us check the readers' reviews on Amazon.com before ordering a book, customers are looking for evidence from those who have experience with a service provider before giving that provider their business. In the past, customers made many provider choices based on brand but, now that the experience (i.e., what a provider puts its customers through) has become so important, today's pickier customer demands proof before partaking in a service offering. It's not surprising that today U.S. consumers report more than 500 billion product/service impressions to one another online every year.[6]

The Perils of Value Migration

In our imagined Service Museum, the pinnacle of service greatness would have been customer satisfaction. Displays might include billboards or advertising pitches featuring language like "Satisfaction guaranteed," "Your satisfaction is our number one goal" or "We are #1 in customer satisfaction." Back then, satisfaction was the ticket to high praise, robust profits, and repeat business. Today, unless your organization is the only fish in the pond, using customer satisfaction as the yardstick of success will ultimately lead to disappointment, maybe even failure.

If you look up the definition of "satisfactory" in Webster's really big dictionary, it says "good enough to fulfill a need or requirement." The verb "to satisfy" originates from the Latin word *satisfacere,* which means "enough." It also means "adequate" or "sufficient." And it means "finished, done, no more for me." Today's customers do not put "adequate" and "value" in the same sentence. "Sufficient" is hardly the language of loyalty, commitment, or passion—what organizations need to evoke to make customers deaf to the siren call of the competition.

Now, if you're in the product-making business, satisfaction might be okay; most consumers want their new dishwasher only to do what they expect it to and nothing more. But, when it comes to an experience like service, the customer's definition of what is adequate or sufficient quickly changes. Imagine coming back from a great experience—say your honeymoon—and you answered someone's "How was your honeymoon?" with "It was completely adequate." You'd probably land in the proverbial dog house.

With a service experience, like any other experience, both our emotions and our logic play into our evaluation. Measures of "satisfaction" are often poor predictors of the most important of all customer service goals: getting customers to come back again, purchase more, forgive more, and advocate more. Achieving these goals helps ensure lowered marketing and customer acquisition costs, fewer customer defections, more word-of-mouth recommendations, and ultimately stronger bottom-line growth.

Take it from the Strativity Group's "2010 Consumer Experience Study: Customer Experience Delivers Profitability," which surveyed more than 900 consumers. They found that customers will buy more and pay more for those purchases that also come with a superior customer experience. More than 70 percent of consumers stated that they would increase their purchases with a specific company by 10 percent or more if that business delivered a superior customer experience.[7]

Want more proof? Research conducted in 2010 by RightNow found that 55 percent of over 2,000 consumers surveyed indicated they became a customer of a company because of their reputation for great customer service. Forty percent of consumers began shopping with a competitor solely due to their reputation for a great customer experience. And, 85 percent of consumers indicated they were willing to pay more than the standard price to ensure a superior customer experience.[8]

In their migration toward value, and value only, today's hard-to-please customers also have been spoiled by greatness. The vintage song "How Ya Gonna Keep 'Em Down on the Farm (after They've Seen Paree)?" captures the essence of this issue. In World War I, farm boys went to war and returned changed forever by the charm and color of Paris (or Venice, or Brussels). Suddenly, the mule-powered plow was without allure and necessary chores abruptly monotonous. Customers have experienced the Paree of service and they know great service when they feel it.

Armed with a much higher standard for service quality, they are frequently disappointed. Customers represented in the Service Museum tolerated okay service and fussed only if service was super bad. They were quick to forgive a hiccup. In fact, they were willing to forgive a lot of hiccups before packing up their coins or coconuts and leaving. Not today. No worth, no way. With choices galore and switching costs plummeting, customers are totally uninterested in offerings without obvious value. The moment there is a hiccup that dilutes the value that attracted them, they are plotting their move to a competitor.

Value has also gotten a more precise and personalized meaning because of the 2007–2009 recession. We all know that children of the Great Depression had frugality embedded into their DNA for the remainder of their lives. No one knows how long-lasting will be the lessons learned from the greatest economic scare since the Great Depression. We can guarantee that during the shelf life of this book customers will scrutinize value in a way they never did before 2007. Over 8 million super-value-conscious customers subscribe to *Consumer Reports,* with another 3 million subscribing to the online version.

The Perils of "Self-Service"

An alteration in the service covenant we've already touched on is another big factor underlying customers' picky nature. Customers have been pushed toward self-service. Don't talk with an attendant behind the ticket counter about getting a boarding pass, go to the self-service kiosk. Don't engage in friendly banter with the check-out clerk and bagger at the store, go to the self-service lane and do it yourself. Don't talk with a call center rep about your unique needs, interact with the IVR and push a lot of buttons until you get what you need. On and on it goes. Customers who formerly partnered with people now must go it alone.

E-SIGHT

Self-service isolates customers and removes them from their "co-creators of the experience" role. Their loneliness is like the thirsty traveler who has just gotten a defective beverage from a vending machine in the middle of nowhere. Never remove easy, timely access to full-service if the customer needs it.

What has been the primary driver for this service isolation? The promise was convenience and time-saving, and that has sometimes been delivered. But, if you have ever been stuck in a self-serve check-out lane when the machine cannot read the item's barcode and an employee must come to reprimand or reboot the machine, you begin to question the benefit. If the ticket-counter kiosk cannot find your airline reservation, forcing you to the back of a long line waiting to see a harried, overworked agent, you wonder about the yo-yo who came up with the brilliant idea of automation. Folk hero John Henry should have survived that race, not just won it! (Just Google it!)

The real benefits of the proliferation of all manner of self-service has brought cost savings to the service provider. With the rising cost of wages—for people who, unlike machines, are expense rather than de-preciation items on the balance sheet—cost saving is accomplished by taking people out of the service equation. So, despite the intermittent virtues of convenience and time savings, there is likely a mercenary motivation behind the merchants' persuading us to migrate away from servers toward systems. We consent to the seduction when it helps us; we rebel when it does not. It is the act of rebelling that makes us especially picky, and often prickly.

How many times have you said "I'd rather do it myself because I know it will be done right"? Or done well? When we serve our-selves, we obviously do it right . . . and well. The tricky part is the ease with which that self-service standard is then generalized to every other service encounter. Having spent time in the trenches of self-service, we know how it is done. And, we watch service providers to match their performance to ours when we are on the other side of the service equation.

Rising standards have also been shaped by our new sense of service time. Self-service, when it works as intended, can be much faster than the old-fashioned way. Let's take getting an airline boarding pass. In olden days you went to the ticket counter, waited in line, showed the very friendly agent your driver's license, and got a boarding pass. Today, in the leisure of your home or office, and typically prompted by the airline in an email, you go online and print your own boarding pass. You can even skip the paper part and have the boarding pass sent directly to your smart phone. At the airport, you bypass the ticketing counter and head straight to the security line.

We were participating in a panel discussion at a conference of Fortune 100 CIOs. A senior leader of one of the ten largest banks in the nation asked us, "How can we maximize the profitability and efficiency of our call centers while minimizing the customer's involvement?" Something about the question left us momentarily confused. "Let me make sure I understand you," one of us responded. "You want to remove all of the service out of customer service?" He responded, "Actually, I'd like to take most of the customer out as well!"

Substituting full-service for self-service essentially hides the other side of the service covenant. Remember the famous Wendy's line, "Where's the Beef?" (If you don't know the ad, watch it on YouTube.) The final line in the ad is prophetic: "I don't think there's anybody back there." It epitomizes the one-sidedness of self-service. Before self-service, we could influence, critique, affirm, and help guide the service experience as it unfolded. The service deliverer could adjust, respond, slow down, or leave us alone. It seemed fair. Now, without the capacity to quality-control it in the moment, customers are more cautious and skeptical of the value they receive. It explains why 63 percent of e-commerce customers rate "live web chat" as the most satisfying channel.[9] Live chat says that self-service can be quickly transformed by the customer into full service if the customer determines there's no beef, just a very big bun.

To top it all off, we drag our new "instant service" standard from the self-service world to the auto service center or the doctor's office and find ourselves ticked off if the wait time is more than thirty-four seconds! In fact, we get downright edgy with whatever service person we encounter just because the self-service world has spoiled us. "Why can't you text me before I arrive if you know the doctor is running late!" or "What do you mean a fifteen minute wait! I had a reservation and I am here right now and on time!" Our outbursts are our way of saying to all service providers, "You folks made me this way, now you get to deal with your creation!"

Pampering the Picky

How do you ensure a healthy dose of picky stays on the tranquil side of "dangerous"? Ensure there is always clear and present value. Value goes beyond a great product or a flawless outcome. It always includes a great experience, one that leaves the customer with a positive memory and, potentially, a story to share.

Chip traded in his Motorola flip phone and Blackberry for a brand spanking new iPhone at his neighborhood AT&T store. Warren Burgess was the perfect sales person. But, within a week, Chip's happy scale had dropped from delight to disappointment—the iPhone speaker would not advance past the whisper level. A keynote speech in midtown New York put him a few blocks from the giant Apple store on Fifth Avenue.

 Go to

Sometimes customers have to go through unpleasantries to the service they need—unavoidable wait, required forms, or unfortunate mistakes. Tool #2 provides tips and techniques helpful for dealing with the Picky in most customers. Tool #9 provides ways to make self-service more partner-like.

"I need a genius!" thought Chip. Visions of rapture from the reputation of the Apple Genius bar were dancing in his head as he approached the Genius. Chip bounced his description of the no-sound challenge off the "I've heard this a million times before" expression of the Genius. There were no questions and little eye contact. The Genius seemed impatient to begin his diagnostic wizardry. After ten minutes of checks and tests the Genius announced his verdict: "You have a defective iPhone. You'll have to take it back to the AT&T store where you bought it for a replacement." As Chip backed away from the Genius, he could hear, "Next in line," echoing in the background.

Fast forward to the neighborhood AT&T store the next day. As soon as Warren saw Chip in the waiting area, he beckoned him back to the really smart side of the store. "How's our new iPhone behaving?" he asked, obviously recalling in complete detail the previous week's sale. Warren patiently listened as Chip outlined the problem and his trip to the Genius bar in the giant New York Apple store.

"Before we take a look at how we need to reprimand our misbehaving iPhone, Chip, let me ask you a few questions." Warren laid the iPhone on the counter as if it were getting in the way of his quest for understanding.

"Did you make any changes in the settings after you left the store last week?" asked Warren. His focus was clearly on his customer, not on the product. Three questions later, Chip's answer to "Did you make any changes to the iPhone itself?" brought a smile to Warren's face. "Now, now, Chip, a Blackberry screen protector will not fit on an iPhone. It covers up the speaker!" Peeling off the interloping screen protector, Warren brought perfect sound into the room. As Chip left the AT&T store, he thought, "Apple may have a Genius bar but AT&T stores have Smart bars." And, customer-smart will trump product genius every time!

Fickle

Why Today's Customers Are Capricious

> Worry about being better; bigger will take care of
> itself. Think one customer at a time and take care of
> each one the best way you can.
>
> Gary Comer
> *Founder of Land's End*

John and his wife Katie were driving home to Atlanta on a Sunday evening after watching one of their children play soccer in North Carolina. "We were looking for a good place to stop for dinner after a long day of travel," John said.

> We eagerly exited the Interstate when we spotted an Outback Steakhouse sign. It was a little before 9:30 when we walked up to the front doors. The doors were locked! The restaurant's sign stated closing time on Sunday to be 9:30. All the exterior lights were still on. NOT FAIR!

> Katie quickly located a Longhorn Steakhouse two exits away and called to make sure they were open. She mentioned our disappointment at the Outback to the gentleman answering the phone at the Longhorn. He assured her they were still open, took our name, suggested we take our time, and promised her

they would be waiting for us even if we arrived a bit after their 10 o'clock closing time.

About ten minutes later we were warmly welcomed to the Longhorn Steakhouse by the restaurant's host who jokingly referred to us as the "Outback people." Even though we were one of only two tables at that late hour, we were treated like regulars. Stephen, our server, welcomed us by name, took our drink order promptly while we studied the menu, and reiterated their desire to serve us, even past closing time. The food was great and the service outstanding. Our fantastic experience in not-very-promising circumstances converted us from Outback to Longhorn lovers!

Customers today are a lot like John and Katie. Burned by experiences that fall very short of their very high expectations, they are constantly on guard for another disappointment. As organizations increase their attempts to move them to more impersonal forms of service, they can feel marginalized at best, abandoned and ignored at worst. They watch person-driven service overtaken by machines and question their worth to the organization. Placing a call to an organization important to their life or livelihood all too often gives a dramatic illustration of this traumatic change: "Your call is very important to us. Your wait time will be 25 minutes!"

Why Are Customers So Unpredictable?

We were standing in line getting ready to board a flight at a major airport. As it got closer to boarding time, we watched a fellow passenger approach the gate attendant with a simple request.

"May I please get a receipt for this flight?" she asked in a very polite voice.

"I don't have time for that," the gate agent replied curtly. "I'm getting ready to board this flight. You'll have to go to the service desk across from gate B-25."

"I appreciate that, honestly," the passenger said. "I am a platinum customer with your airline and a trip to the service center on the other side of the terminal will likely cause me to miss this flight."

The other passengers waited for the gate agent's response. Without making eye contact with the passenger-in-need, she picked up her microphone and announced: "Will all passengers needing a little extra time in boarding, please proceed to the jetway!"

There was a time when the definition of loyalty was very clear. We used the phrase "loyal customer" to refer to those who purchased more (and more frequently), stayed away from the competition, forgave us when we made mistakes, and told friends or colleagues about their experience. Today loyalty is defined simply as "a customer who returns." Only super-loyal advocates exhibit the behaviors and practices formerly reserved for loyalists.

Accenture reports that 69 percent of consumers indicated leaving at least one provider last year due to poor service—up from 49 percent just five years ago. And 62 percent of respondents in the Accenture research who left their providers during the past twelve months did so because of the poor quality of the service experience they received. Respondents who said their service expectations were frequently disappointing were the most likely to leave.[1]

WHAT BRAND?

The number of customers choosing "a brand I can trust" as the most important attribute for selecting a company has fallen 9 percent to 10 percent a year for the last two years.

Convergys
2010 Scorecard Research

According to Convergys research, 85 percent of customers who call themselves loyal to an organization are not necessarily demonstrating loyalty in the ways we have historically considered loyal. The research found that only 29 percent of "loyal" customers indicate they would forgive a single bad experience and still continue doing business with a company. What's more, only 10 percent of those who labeled themselves as "loyal" remained loyal after a bad experience.[2] Look at the retail industry as an example. Accenture research suggests that 70 percent of U.S. customers are faithful to one retailer.[3] However further study reveals that 85 percent of these "loyal" customers will shop elsewhere if properly enticed. And what does it take to entice these "loyal" customers? Sixty two percent say they will defect for better prices![4]

Loyal customers today are less forgiving than they used to be. Convergys research shows that, after reporting a bad experience, 47 percent of customers stop doing business with the company. While 49 percent to 70 percent of customers indicate they are very or extremely loyal to a company, compared to 2008 they are 6 percent to 27 percent less likely to exhibit loyalty in a number of measureable ways. For example, they now are 27 percent less likely to state they make frequent purchases of a company's products and 19 percent less likely to participate in loyalty programs. Customers were 6 percent less likely to agree that loyalty means they forgive one bad experience and continue doing business with a company (29 percent down from 31 percent).[5]

What is the message? It takes a lot of delighting experiences to foster loyalty, far more than it once did. But it only takes one less-than-satisfying experience to destroy that loyalty. Loyalty comes slowly on foot but it flees on a fast horse!

Anxious Customers on the Trust High Wire

We live our lives on promises. From the time we are children grasping the concept of "cross my heart and hope to die," we all need a proof of trust as we wait for a promise to be kept. From "Scout's honor" to "I do" to "the whole truth and nothing but the truth," we seek cues that allay our worries. Lifeguards, the bus schedule, and even the uniformed security guard at the bank, are promises waiting to be kept.

Customer service begins with a promise made or implied. Promises sound like "We'll be landing on time," "It will be ready by noon," or "Your order will be shipped right away." The trust gap is the emotional space between hope and evidence, between expectation and fulfillment. Trust is the emotion that propels customers to the other side of the gap. The manner in which an organization manages the trust gap drives every other component of the service encounter. As one frequent flyer said, "No matter how friendly the flight attendant, how delicious the meal, or how comfortable the seat, if the plane lands in the wrong city or four hours late, I am not a happy camper." Granted, great service recovery can turn an aggrieved customer back into a satisfied customer. But the residue of betrayal will leave a disappointed customer perpetually on guard for the next letdown.

You cannot avoid the trust gap when making or intimating a promise to a customer—you can only manage it. Insecurity and doubt are essential features of the trust gap. But, requiring customers to walk on the high wire of faith is an inescapable fact of every service encounter.

As customers, our journey across that high wire of faith is a trip with or without anguish based solely on the net of trust the service provider extends to support the passage. Customers' perception of that net of trust makes all the difference in how they grade their experiences. No net, no loyalty; shaky net, no loyalty. To ease their anxiety, we must deal with several factors that have made the trip across that wire a trip that today's customers are reluctant to take.

The Power of Trust Cues

Paramount to customers' prudence in navigating the high wire is the removal of the net. Shifting customers from full service to self-service has shaken their confidence in the guardian of the net. Notice how the IVR forces you, as a customer eager to spend money, to use their language. Were there a person at the helm, there would be the capacity to interpret your nod or "uh-huh" as meaning yes. The sheer aloneness of automated service has eliminated compassion for the customer, since we all know the computer cannot be programmed to care.

E-SIGHT

Today's customers are a lot like a frequently jilted lover. They can detect deception and disappointment a mile away. Never give them a reason to worry about being betrayed.

The customer's confidence in a service provider relies on cues of trust. These are the signals that promote assurance. It's a high-wire walk when you see the shaking hands of a nurse about to extract your blood, or a letter other than A on the health certificate displayed on the restaurant's wall, or the unprofessional appearance of the website asking for your credit card information. Significantly reduce any of the cues of trust, and you leave the customer less willing to entrust their loyalty.

Now, take a quick trip down memory lane. Think back to a boy-friend or girlfriend in high school or college. Recall the beginning of that relationship. How skeptical were you when the chosen one was seen in deep conversation with someone you did not know? How many phone calls did you overhear when your first question after the call ended was "Who was that?" Did you ever eavesdrop, check the last few emails on the person's PDA or phone, or ask a best friend what others were saying about your relationship?

We can chalk this silliness up to the insecurity of puppy love. But, the search for cues of trust in that relationship was driven by exactly the same kind of anxiety customers now exhibit. Self-service, service automation, reliance on experts, and declining value have robbed us of many of the vital trust cues we could "spot across the dance floor." With diminished means of picking up the cues, we become capricious, fickle, and hesitant to place our faith in a favorite service provider.

Expectation Anxiety

Anxiety about getting on the high wire has also been exacerbated by the customer's history of previous "falls." Part of their disappointment comes from climbing expectations. Customer expectations, gorged by their experiences with the occasional great service provider, have raised the standard for what must be at the other end of the wire to make their trip worthwhile. They have been over-stimulated daily by the Internet and other communications media. Television has become high-definition and multi-media. The nightly news has the weather,

ball scores, stock market reports, and a crawling headline simultaneously on the screen. Internet servers have become a haven for colorful ads with streaming video while you try to concentrate on your emails. Such steady arousal has made a simple hotel check-in, taking the dog to the vet, or grocery shopping seem humdrum.

The flip side of the expectations effect on customers' standards for service is that their experiences have too often left them disappointed. Fighting to hold on to razor-thin margins, organizations have cut staff to the bone. Their cost-cutting attempts to use cheaper but less-skilled

employees, coupled with piling more duties on the employees left after RIFs, have presented customers with an apathetic, "deer-in-the-
headlights" front line, more eager to lie low or clock out than deliver
a superior experience. It's no surprise that silent attrition is a growing
issue for all organizations.

Convergys research found that customers who do not report their
bad experiences stop doing business with the company 34 percent of
the time. Overall, 12 percent of customers who had a bad experience
did not report it and stopped doing business with a company.[7] Companies have pushed customers to lower-cost channels, worked to contain them in self-help channels, migrated them to cheaper off-shore/
near-shore support, and emphasized quick resolutions that repaired
problems but left the customer relationship broken.

Granted, organizations must balance the service that customers
might love with the service the bottom line can withstand. It's possible
to serve your way to bankruptcy. The key is helping customers to have
realistic expectations regarding the level of service their revenue can
fund (what is reasonable at the price)—as well as communicating a
path for them to journey to feature-rich service that is in sync with the
"revenue-rich funding" customers are willing to provide. While airline
passengers all expect good service no matter what they paid for their
tickets, they do not expect first-class perks in the economy seats.

Service-providing organizations also too frequently forget the pattern-making components of the customer's mind. We are all creatures
of patterns. We search for patterns to help us understand our world. If
we see a "Bridge Out" sign on the highway, we do not have to drive off
the cliff to know what the sign means. Words and symbols carry much
deeper meaning because of the patterns they represent. Watergate is
more than a place in D.C., 9-11 is more than a date on the calendar,
and Christmas is more than a winter holiday. We have elaborate patterns that help us shortcut our way to understanding. When we hear
a familiar tune, it is a pattern—one that is well enough established in
our mind to know when a wrong note is played.

Pattern making enables us to make quick predictions. Like the

Bridge Out example, if a situation in which we have been many times begins to look as if it may turn dark, we mentally complete the pattern and escape before having to experience the ending.

Given customers' impatience with service, their mental storehouse of disappointing service experiences, and their pattern-making protection machine, even the hint of service gone awry can send them off to visit a competitor. It is for this reason that negative customer reviews on a website have such a powerful viral impact. Not wanting to risk investing their limited funds in a potentially bad outcome, customers read the review and opt to look elsewhere without even giving the subject of the review a try.

No matter how much an organization believes they create and sustain a "You can trust us" approach, it is what customers believe that counts. Smart organizations—those that retain the best customers for the longest time—understand the trust gap can never be taken for granted. It must be treated as precarious, since it can be shattered with a single malfunction, misunderstanding, or mishap. It must be eternally monitored because a single snarky review or casual downbeat comment from a friend can turn the green light red, sending the customer in another direction.

The Message in the Meaning

The "fickle" label for today's customers was selected to characterize their propensity to play the field, always in search of value they can trust. It symbolizes the customer perpetually on guard, suspicious that any tiny service hiccup is just the front edge of another large disappointment. And, it denotes the haste with which customers depart and their unwillingness to stay around to give a service provider a second chance. Contemporary wisdom suggests building up the customers' storehouse of trust through repeated reminders of promises kept, in order to increase the chances the potentially fickle customer will say "I'll stay with you."

Most customers would prefer to be labeled "selective" rather than "capricious" or "fickle." Being careful in our choice-making helps bring quality and value to the commerce of service. But, the not-so-nice component of "fickle" can bring uncertainty and gaminess to an otherwise healthy encounter. Great service providers enjoy customers that keep them on their toes; few like customers who are spoiled. Keeping on the good side of fickle requires ensuring an experience fortified with trust.⁻

"When people ask me how do you make it in show business," says famed actor Steve Martin, "what I always tell them (and nobody ever takes note of it 'cuz it's not the answer they wanted to hear—what they want to hear is here's how you get an agent, here's how you write a script, here's how you do this, but I always say) 'Be so good they can't ignore you.' If somebody's thinking, 'How can I be really good?' people are going to come to you. It's much easier doing it that way than going to cocktail parties."[8]

Service customers' trust is all about being really good. It means customers experiencing you making a focus on "being really good" your top priority.

Go to

Customers who are fickle typically lack the trust needed to form longer term relationships with service providers. Tool #6 includes a list of techniques for creating the kind of emotional connection that nurtures customer confidence and trust.

Fancying the Fickle

"Good morning! Welcome to our *USA Today* route. Now, if I should go completely brain dead and miss you, please don't hesitate to call me at the number below. I will personally re-deliver your paper as soon as possible. If you have a complaint that you and I can't solve, you may call my district manager directly. His name and number are also below. Thanks a lot. We really appreciate your business."

A neighbor got this letter along with his first *USA Today* home delivery. It was crafted, copied and conveyed by Hazel, the local newspaper delivery person. Take a look at its tone and information! Research shows the number one concern of customers of home delivery newspapers is "not getting a paper."[9] Hazel's letter deals with that loyalty driver right up front, and it gives the distinct impression that you and your business are truly valued.

Great service is not rocket surgery! It is simply making your customers matter deeply and carefully managing all the details important to them. It is earning and retaining their respect as you nurture their loyalty, never taking them for granted. It is always being a "Hazel" with maintaining a laser focus on being really good on behalf of customers.

CHAPTER 4

Vocal

Why Today's Customers Are Noisy

> If you make customers unhappy in the physical
> world, they might each tell six friends. If you make
> customers unhappy on the Internet, they can each
> tell 6,000 friends.
>
> Jeff Bezos, Founder and CEO
> *Amazon.com*

Insight came from a late night game of "Trivial Pursuit Goes to the Movies." It was being played by a group of business leaders after drinks and dinner at the two-day retreat we were facilitating. The object of the game was for one team to read a famous movie line and for the opposing team to name the movie in which it was spoken and the actor who said it. The one with the most answers at the end of the deck would be the winner.

"What we've got here is a failure to communicate," one team member read from the card. Before anyone on the other team could give the correct answer (Strother Martin in *Cool Hand Luke**), some-

---

* *Cool Hand Luke* is a 1968 movie produced by Jalem Productions and based on the novel written by Donn Pearce.

one on that team shouted "Revenge of the Customers!" It was a humorous response, and very prophetic! Consider the following facts:

- While 95 percent of firms surveyed indicate they collect customer information, only 10 percent actually "deploy" a change in policy based on customer feedback. And, only 5 percent of firms tell customers that they used their feedback.[1]

- When thousands of customers were asked if organizations listened, 39 percent indicated companies do not listen to or act on customer feedback. Yet, 87 percent of employees and executives believed "we listen."[2]

- When executives of over two hundred companies were asked if they provided a "superior experience," 80 percent indicated that they did. However, only 8 percent of their customers agreed with them.[3]

- Doctors, on average, after asking a patient the initial symptom-describing question, interrupt that patient within the first 18 seconds of the answer.[4]

Lots of talking, not much communicating! Ever had a maitre d', host, waiter, or waitress saunter up to your table and ask the ubiquitous "How's everything?" And, even though you were unimpressed by the food, underwhelmed by the service, and annoyed by delays, you said "Fine." Congratulations! You have participated in one of the most meaningless efforts in modern business—useless feedback solicitation with no real pursuit of understanding.

What the restaurant learned from your "fine" is not only irrelevant; it's probably not true! The frontline employee thinks he has heard an actual evaluation of the meal and the service. The customer thinks she's just given a generic response—"Good morning, how are you?" And, management thinks they have another happy customer.

What we've got here is a failure to communicate. When customers with something important to say don't get heard, they get even more vocal—and louder. And when that fails, they talk with someone who will listen—their friends. Suddenly websites proliferate with customer reviews and Facebook accounts exceed 500 million people, each with an average of 130 friends.

Ironically, the storyline of the movie *Cool Hand Luke* featured a prisoner (played by Paul Newman) who refused to conform to life in a rural prison. Customers are registering their refusal to play along with poor service by lighting up the Internet board and getting all their friends and family to play along with them.

MOUSE TRUMPS MOUTH

Remember: Social media drives five times the impact of traditional word-of-mouth. The average post is read by 45 people.

Convergys
2010 Scorecard Research

The Impact of Customer Noise

If you went to the customer feedback section of our Service Museum, you would find a very limited display. There would be a few almost empty suggestion boxes, a survey too long to complete in less than a week, and a returns department with an iron-fisted sourpuss firmly in charge. The conventional wisdom in the halls of the museum would be that one only hears from the really happy or the really incensed customer. The fact was, the silent majority—and, a very large majority at that—made up the bulk of customers served by any organization.

Fast forward to today and you have a much higher decibel level on customer discontent. The arithmetic on the "happy customers tell three people; unhappy ones tell ten" has multiplied geometrically. As Jeff Bezos warns at the opening of this chapter, customers can tell thousands through the outreach capacity of the Internet. Today "customer-generated media," especially via the Internet, has dramatically increased customers' ability to tell stories about their experiences with those who serve them. This once-nerdy path has morphed into an information freeway, dramatically escalating the customer's power and capacity to influence other customers. As author Pete Blackshaw says, "To live in a world where consumers now control the conversation and where satisfied customers tell three friends while angry customers tell 3,000, companies must achieve credibility on every front."[5]

Who's talking? For the first time in history (at least the first time in a long time), most customers are assertively voicing their concerns. Some research shows that of the almost 60 percent of customers having had a bad experience in the last year, 66 percent told someone at the company and 80 percent told a friend or colleague.[6] The silent majority is no longer silent. When the pocketbook gets squeezed, customers are more vocal about letting someone know when they do not get value. Customers at the end of the 2007–2009 recession were 14 percent more likely to complain than before the recession.[7]

In another study, 79 percent of customers who had a negative experience told others about it, according to the "Customer Experience Report North America 2010" from RightNow.com and Harris Interactive. Eighty-five percent wanted to warn others about the pitfalls of doing business with that company; 66 percent wanted to discourage others from buying from that company. On top of that, 76 percent indicated word of mouth influenced their purchasing decisions.[8]

In addition to saying something, customers have another vocal tactic when they have a bad experience—they leave! Convergys reports that 44 percent of customers stop doing business immediately and another 15 percent exit as soon as their contract is up![9] Other researchers found that 82 percent of consumers quit doing business with a company because of a bad customer experience, up from 59 percent four years ago.[10] Think about that. Over half of customers with a bad experience go elsewhere.

Today social media drives five times the impact of traditional word of mouth. And, now for the biggest wakeup call: the viral effect. Over 60 percent of customers who hear about a bad experience on social media stop doing business with or avoid doing business with the offending company.[11] This "secondary smoke" phenomenon will grow as the use of social media increases and more and more consumers are digital natives, not digital immigrants.

Can You Hear Me Now?

Vincent Ferrari decided to close his AOL account. Having heard friends describe the nightmare it could be, he elected to tape the conversation. After all, he reasoned, the phone message customers get at the beginning of the call is, "Your call may be recorded." The simple request—"cancel my account"—turned into a nightmare as the very polite call center rep kept ignoring his request and attempted to change his mind. The more the response to Ferrari's service cancellation request escalated to a hard-sell pitch, the more the rep sounded like a bully. This went on for an excruciatingly long time.

Ferrari was so frustrated by the call that he posted the audio conversation on YouTube. Within days the video was seen by hundreds of thousands of people. NBC picked up the human interest story and brought Vincent on the show . . . and, played the tape! Check out the story today on YouTube and you will be one of more than 500,000 viewers to witness what Vincent endured with AOL.[12]

Now, let's look at the other side of this corrupted service covenant. In a blog on "The Consumerist" website, Ben Popken wrote:

> For "John," the call center employee heard on the tape, to deploy the kind of mental warfare heard on the tape, he had to be well-trained. A plain manila envelope arrived on our desk this week. Inside was the 81-page "Enhanced Sales Training for AOL Retention Consultants" manual. Upon opening, the flowchart, "Guide to a World-Class Retention Call," fell out.

> It's amazing that the story has come this far, that Vincent could record his attempt to cancel AOL, that recording would shoot to national TV, and now, a mole has sent us incriminating company documents. One thing quickly becomes evident after reading the pages of tips and tactics. Callers are viewed not as customers, but prospects. Under the heading, "Think of Cancellation Calls as Sales Leads," the manual reads:

> If you stop and think about it, every Member that calls in to cancel their account is a hot lead. Most other sales jobs require

you to create your own leads, but in the Retention Queue the
leads come to you! Be eager to take more calls, get more leads
and close more sales. More leads mean more selling opportunities for you and cost savings for AOL.[13]

Popken continues in his blog:

> In a public statement, AOL's Nicholas Graham claimed that
> John "violated our customer service guidelines and practices,
> and everything that AOL believes to be important in customer
> care—chief among them being respect for the member, and
> swiftly honoring their requests." If this is true, then why is there
> such a complex system designed to thwart those very requests?
> Brevity thrives on simplicity.[14]

What's Made Customers So Noisy

Why are customers so vocal today? There are surface reasons. For one,
organizations more actively solicit feedback than before. How many
surveys (snail-mailed, emailed, or phone-called) have you received in
the last month? Get your car serviced and the service rep will tell you
to expect a call from J.D. Power. Clerks in stores remind you of the
800-Ticked-Off number at the bottom of the sales receipts. Plus, the
Internet has made it much easier to voice an opinion. Finish a transaction online and the service provider wants to switch you quickly
to a survey form.

More and more companies today are trying to get an "Academy
Award." Getting on a big-deal list or winning an honor brings pub-
licity and added revenue. Some organizations have entire units that
do nothing but prepare nomination and application forms for special
awards. Obviously, customer evaluations are a key part of that effort.

But these are superficial explanations for the rise of the noisy customer. The real question is: why are customers motivated to give their
two cents' worth? The answer springs from the great service covenant
shift. The transformation of service from getting service through a
partner-like, egalitarian relationship to becoming the "subject" of an

"expert" has left many customers disenfranchised. It has fueled an assertiveness never before seen in the streets of commerce. Some label this forcefulness "restless"; others, the victims of customer venom, would call it downright dangerous. With customer participation removed from the service equation, there is more and more backlash and whiplash, and less and less of what we'd call "dinner on the ground" for customers. Let's examine that last concept more closely.

E-SIGHT

Automating a relationship is like visiting the Grand Canyon online. It may look and sound the same, but it can never feel the same. Never take the R out of CRM (customer relationship management).

"Dinner on the ground" was code for community in small Southern towns when we were growing up. While this naturally applied to all family reunions, its most special form occurred after certain church services. "Dinner on the ground" was a super opportunity for little boys to run, holler, and pull ponytails, pretty much unsupervised since their caretakers were occupied with set-up and clean-up. For the women, it was a time to show off a new recipe; men told tales over sweet iced tea of the one that got away. Everyone went home stuffed and happy after eating way too much fried chicken and peach pie.

This "everyone brings something" event brought people closer and enabled them to feel their interdependence. It was community in its purest form. The covenant was egalitarian. It was a sad day when someone got the bright idea of "just calling Big Al and having him bring barbecue with all the trimmings." The "expert" cook made it all much easier. It also completely removed the recipients from getting to "vote" on how it all would unfold.

Customers' feelings about a service provider soar when they get a chance to put skin in the game. Inclusion not only captures the creativity and competence of customers as they serve *with* you but it also elevates their commitment and allegiance. People care when they share. Wise service providers attract customer loyalty by making the "dinner on the ground" side of service as fun, memorable, and wholesome as a church picnic. But, when bringing a lemon icebox pie is taken from the Susies and Steves and given to the Big Als, something breaks in the customer's notion of the service covenant.

We were working in Baltimore and staying in a new hotel whose brand was touted to be the latest in contemporary hotel hospitality. Check-in was kiosk-driven. There was no front desk staff, something we value because of their capacity to help tailor our experience. Instead, there was a single person behind a circular counter in the middle of the lobby. However, it was clear this young server was more of an exceptions concierge. He was so overwhelmed with multi-tasking that he was very slow getting us checked in since we refused to use the kiosk approach. Rather than adapting to the obvious road-warrior guests he was serving, he spoke in text-message lingo and the new techno-babble. "Later, dude" replaced "Thank you"; IDK replaced "Let me find someone who can answer that question."

The funkiness went on. The gift shop had been transformed into a collection of vending machines. The lobby bar, no doubt crafted to be high-energy, to us was actually high-noise, sending a cacophony through the lobby that made it difficult to have a focused conversation. The guest-room desk was littered with cool electronic devices but with no guides on how to use them. Even though we are early-adopters, we felt out of place and out of date as we witnessed hospitable service become hostile service.

We Are Stronger When We Are Connected

Vice Admiral Jim Stockdale was one of the most decorated officers in the history of the U.S. Navy. A Medal of Honor recipient, he served as president of the Naval War College and later as president of The Citadel. But, ask the person on the street about Stockdale, and many will remember him only as a Vietnam prisoner-of-war for over seven years or for his fifteen minutes of fame as Ross Perot's running mate in the 1992 presidential campaign, when he seemed out of place in the vice-presidential debate against the polished political pizzazz of Al Gore and Dan Quayle. Few knew that Stockdale had had only one week to prepare, while the other two debaters had been preparing for over twenty years!

Before we go any further with Admiral Stockdale's story it is important to know that we did not include it as sort of a literary intermission. Stockdale's plight, while dramatic and extreme, has features similar to the isolation customers sometimes feel when relegated to the Internet for their service requirements. More important, the way Stockdale and his colleagues effectively coped with the circumstance has a fascinating and chilling parallel to the explosion of social media. Sue Shellenbarger writes in the *Wall Street Journal,* "Constantly connected via Facebook and Twitter, you may feel like you have a lot of friends. But will they be your go-to friends in a crisis? Overwhelmed by home, family and work obligations . . . these connections are the kind that best support health and happiness."[15] Now let's return to the Admiral's story.

The jet aircraft Stockdale piloted during the Vietnam War was shot down over enemy territory and he was immediately captured. He would spend the next seven-and-a-half years in the Hoa Lo prison in North Vietnam. He was one of eleven prisoners separated from the others and placed in solitary confinement in the cruelest section of the prison. Their cells measured three by nine feet, slightly larger than the average grave, illuminated by a single light bulb that was never turned off. They were beaten during the day and constrained with ankle irons at night. Despite the fact that his leg was shattered, his shoulder dislocated, and several spinal disks smashed as a result of the plane crash, Stockdale was the most severely tortured.

There were strict rules about no communication between prisoners. Isolated and disenfranchised, the eleven prisoners worked out ways to connect and communicate. They tapped codes to each other and placed their tin cups against the walls to pick up tapping vibrations. Secret hand signals, abbreviations, and acronyms communicated to one another all helped each prisoner know that, though confined, he was not alone.

Despite the fact that they were sometimes separated by an

empty cell or non-adjoining walls, silent contact never stopped for more than a day before they figured out a brand new way to communicate. Their captors were puzzled and amazed by the resilience and emotional strength of the prisoners led by Admiral Stockdale.[16]

Like Admiral Stockdale, when customers lose their village and are isolated from service providers bent on taking the server out of service, they respond by creating their own village. When you "own" your village, you nurture it and never take it for granted—just like you might a real village with shops and parks and Main Street. With the Internet, the formerly isolated customer now has a tin cup to place against the walls to listen for tapping from their very own community.

When the service covenant is altered without our consent or contribution, customers turn their disenfranchisement into influence and, like Stockdale, subject their captors (the organization) to their will and authority. Customers now rule! And, wired customers with a bone to pick and an ax to grind are ready, willing, and able to wield that power at any merchant who shackles them with poor quality or an inferior service experience. Ask Maytag! A power blogger with over a million followers, Heather Armstrong (http://dooce.com), cut a sizeable dent into Maytag's reputation (and likely their bottom line) simply by advising her followers to "boycott Maytag."[17] Vocal does not mean that customers speak up. It means they bring a decibel level to their voice that mobilizes others to action.

Look at the popularity of customer review sites like Yelp.com, epinions.com, Citysearch.com, and Angieslist.com; a major part of Amazon.com's popularity is the customer reviews section of the website. Recent research demonstrates how quickly customers have turned up the volume and come to depend on others' experiences to assist them in making decisions about which providers to choose. For example:

- 59 percent of customers use social media to vent anger about their experience

- 72 percent sometimes research a provider's customer-care reputation online before purchasing and 62 percent stop or avoid using that provider based on results

- 84 percent consider a provider's customer-care quality when deciding whether to do business with a company
- 74 percent choose some providers based on other customers' service experience[18]

Having constructed their own community linked together around common interests, customers now have a connection with their crowd to replace the one they lost with all too many companies. The Internet has elevated the importance of the cyber watering hole to far more than what we think of as simply social media. The label "social" implies a chat room for swapping recipes and baseball trivia. But, the cyber watering hole is now the crucible for gaining a deeper understanding of matters that matter, a forum to create instantaneous communal attention to a subject of significance, and a source for staying on the cutting edge of forces that impact the community and its members.

"Vocal" is the energy behind every grassroots initiative. It is the viral feature that influences and incites just as it educates and excites. It can be a link that brings friends together like a family reunion or "dinner on the ground." It can be a bulletin board of helpful and healthy comments that make negotiating commerce much easier and much more valuable. But, in the hands of restless, aggravated customers, it can also be a force that mobilizes frustration and channels their concern to a village of like-minded citizens. Facebook, crafted to be a place for cyber pen pals, can become "In Your Face book" and tweets can become the drumbeats that provide a wakeup call as well as a means to marshal others to track and trail.

Revering the Vocal

It is fascinating that singing has been used as an alert or warning phrase. Think of the canary in the coal mine or the saying "It's not over 'til the fat lady sings." When customers "sing" it can be a cry for communication. Great service providers encourage customer singing. The song is more than important feedback and intelligence, it represents the sense of community that customers have watched being gradually removed from the service covenant. That hunger for community is innate for 99.9 percent of customers.

As customers, we all enjoy the convenience of online engagement. Vocalization (via face-to-face, ear-to-ear, or word of mouse) is what makes us social animals. Furthermore, extroverts who "talk to think" outnumber introverts who "think to talk" by four to one.[19] One of the most important stages in the evolution of *Homo sapiens* was the emergence of food-growers (not just nomadic hunters and gatherers). The grower stage led to the advancement of a social order, culture, and progress. In some ways the Internet has made us more like lone hunters again; the emergence of social media may be a manifestation of the gatherer in us seeking a voice for "singing."

Go to

Vocal customers want to be heard and valued. Their venting to friends sometimes happens because they feel ignored or unappreciated by a service provider. Tool #7 and Tool #8 outline ways to better understand what is important to customers.

Vocal means more than simply fostering good communication. It means creating and valuing a village or community. When service providers and customers unite in the village of commerce the service covenant is strong and intact. A solid covenant requires service providers connecting with customers in a fashion that is like a partner, not a mercenary; it is more about a relationship than a transaction.

Take it from New Mexico Tea Company owner David Edwards. David was staring at bankruptcy and needed a six-month loan to get him from slow summer sales to a profitable December. An SBA loan would take months, the bank turned him down, and he needed cash fast. He turned to his customers for help. He created a clever gift card that could be purchased on PayPal—a $50 gift card purchased in the summer but held until December could be used to buy $55 worth of tea. A $100 gift card bought $115 worth. The micro-lending concept was a huge success. And the big payoff was that after David's partnering gesture his loyal customers felt even more loyal than before.[20]

CHAPTER 5

Vain

Why Today's Customers Are Self-Centered

There are two kinds of egotists: Those who admit it,
and the rest of us.

Laurence J. Peter
The Peter Principle

It recently made business headlines: The most popular brand in the world focused on the experience, not just on their long-famous product. Coca-Cola introduced their "Freestyle" vending machine.[1] Their ad copy described the machine as "all packaged in an innovative and interactive fountain experience." The machine was designed with help from automobile manufacturer Ferrari! Step one, pick your favorite Coke beverage—Fanta, Sprite, Minute Maid lemonade, Coke Zero, or whatever. Step two, pick your favorite flavoring. Want a raspberry-flavored Coke, a peach-flavored Fanta, or coconut-flavored lemonade? More than a hundred combinations are possible. The vending machine fills a plastic cup with ice and your special concoction.

Now, here is the best part. At the end of the day the vending fountain electronically sends all the combinations chosen to the R&D unit at Coca-Cola headquarters. By watching patterns of purchases, Coca-Cola is able to introduce new products tailored precisely to customers' latest whims. Who knows, a revolutionary new Coke product may be coming

It's tough being a player in the self-serve age.

to your zip code soon! So, what's the point? If the Coke vending machine down the street can do that, what will your customers expect next?

Customers gravitate toward service providers skilled at focusing on exactly what they want, when they want it, and the way they want it. This "all about me" at its worst might be pure selfishness. At its most wholesome, it can be as enriching as your significant other remembering your birthday—or your aunt forgoing another tie to give you for Christmas the first edition of a book you have been hunting.

Let's examine two other service examples. USAA is the highly popular financial services company with a special market niche—active or retired military and their families. They introduced an iPhone application that lets their customers (members) deposit a check anytime, from anywhere. The customer endorses the check, takes an iPhone photo of both sides, and sends it to USAA for instant credit. The catalyst for the new app? Customer input and feedback! Managers listen to all customer voicemail feedback and review all automated customer satisfaction surveys.

America's e-marketplace, eBay, has introduced a new iPhone app that lets you buy and sell from anywhere using your cell phone. In the first month of the eBay app introduction, there were 5 million downloads and over $500 million in transactions.[2] Some guy bought an antique Corvette, probably while waiting in the parking lot for his kids to come out of McDonald's. "When you have 84 million active users, any time you make a change, someone is going to be upset," said CEO John Donahoe. "But we listen and we incorporate their feedback with what we believe is best for the collective good of the marketplace."[3]

Customer expectations have been rising for years. Customers want service faster, cheaper, and without a hassle. They enjoy the convenience of online self-service. But, they want the experience to feel that it was respectfully designed with people in mind, not just as a cost-cutting measure or for the convenience of the company. Should things go differently than expected, customers want a back-door to a helpful, smart partner to guide them through the challenge.

With the advent of sophisticated computer and telecommunications advances plus just-in-time manufacturing, organizations have taught customers they can "Have it your way." "We are so used to customizing the world around us . . . to being able on Facebook to customize our wall and to create who we are, and technology has powered that," notes Amy Manitis, vice president of marketing at Cafe-Press.com, in a *Wall Street Journal* article.[4] Long gone is the Henry Ford-like sentiment: "Customers can have any color automobile they like as long as it's black." The more organizations offer a wide array of tailor-made service choices, the more one-size-fits-all approaches look way out-of-date.

Great service today requires understanding the self-centered customer and rethinking the time-place-process of how you deliver service to customers. BMW took customers' vanity and their self-centered expectations to new heights with their Mini Cooper. New owners got adoption papers when they plunked down a deposit to buy a new Mini. It came with a means to go online and watch their specific Mini being "born" on the factory assembly line. Lately they have made news with their special billboards in major cities that respond to a radio-frequency identification (RFID) tag or chip embedded in the owner's BMW key fob. Ride by the billboard and it will flash, "Hi, Susan, nice day for your red convertible" or any other message Susan may choose.[5]

Wynn Puts the "Us" Back in Customer

Consultant and author Ben McConnell shares a great example of how the Wynn Hotel in Las Vegas brings personalization to the experience of guests.

> First, the hotel has upgraded the lowly swipe card room key and personalized it by putting my name on it. (Well, not my full name—they thought better of the wisdom of a guest's entire name on a room card.) That's bound to appeal to guests who love to collect stuff with their name on it, especially if the room key is a memento of a memorable time. Once inside my room, I noticed my room phone also displayed my name. I must be in the right room. Finally, when I turned on the flat-screen TV, there was my name again. Not only did I know I was in the right room (in previous experiences, I've had at least two hotels book me into occupied rooms), but I liked how the hotel recognized me several times, but not in a creepy way.[6]

If you haven't had the experience of a stranger swiping a key card and bursting into your hotel room, or of you being the one to walk in on someone, the Wynn approach may not hold the significance it does for many road warriors. But we all enjoy being addressed by our name and never seem to tire of hearing it or seeing it. Starbucks does a wonderful job with this by writing your name on your cup and saying it out loud several times in the process of making your customized drink. Customers today love this personalized experience.

The Origin of Customer Vanity

As customers, when we look in the mirror we don't see a narcissistic, self-important person looking back. Yet, let a hidden camera catch us in a store, and we may see someone frustrated with a frontline person who fails to remember our specifics on our second visit. We see a person annoyed if asked to repeat any information already given to the first call center rep. And, we hold suspect any organization that treats us as the "next in line," someone ordinary or just like everyone else.

Narcissism takes its name from Greek mythology. Narcissus was a good looking dude who was clueless about what he looked like. One day, walking in the woods, he got thirsty and stopped at a pool of water to have a drink. When he saw his reflection, not understanding the mirror effect of water (go figure!), he assumed it was another person and began speaking to the handsome image in the water. Hiding behind a nearby tree, a nymph named Echo, under a curse whereby she always has the final word, was forced to repeat every word she heard Narcissus say to the image in the pool. He thought the reflection was speaking to him and eventually fell in love with it. Unable to attract his love, Narcissus pouted by the pool and was ultimately transformed into the flower that bears his name. So, the word narcissism has come to mean self-love—a moderate amount of which is deemed necessary for effective goal-oriented behavior, but an extreme amount is considered an indication of insecurity.

Narcissism can help us to understand today's customer. Alter a customer's capacity to influence the participative side of the co-creation called service and you naturally get a backlash of some sort. Strip out the component of the service covenant that enables customers to monitor or regulate their experience as it is unfolding, and you get apprehension. Relegate the customer's participation to dependence on an expert and you get a prescription for service insecurity. Isolate the customers from the experience by downgrading their participation to interaction with a machine with no link to a person and, like Narcissus, the customers "pout by the pool" and transform their allegiance into defiance.

But there's more. When service is personalized, it reminds customers they are still vitally present in the service equation. Having one's name on it or needs embedded in it informs the customer that they are considered a valued recipient of the offering, not a common end-user.

Think of customer service as being like choosing ornaments for a Christmas tree. If you decorate enough Christmas trees over a long enough time, at some point you discover that almost all of the ornaments on the front of the tree are handmade or have some special meaning. Destined for the back branches are those store-bought ones that looked pleasing to the eye but have no shortcut to the heart. The special ones all have stories attached; the store-bought ones just have hooks.

From the customer point of view, the service experience is a lot like picking out ornaments for the tree. The customer might start out settling for what looks good, what's convenient, or what is the least expensive. But, sooner or later most customers want handmade service—personalized to their specs—with a story they can share with others. The glitz might not be there but the value surely is.

I'll Have It My Way

Today's customers want it "my way." Customers in the past were okay with generic, one-size-fits-all, generalized everything. Now customers want more than brand specific—they want "me specific"! Everything should be personalized. Amazon and NetFlix monitor our buying patterns to suggest-sell only what fits what customers like. We abhor junk mail and spam specifically because they fail the monogram test. Business-to-business customers expect all vendors to know their unique requirements and to present only solutions that scratch their exclusive customer itch. We get agitated when the Best Buy geek or Apple genius fails to recognize us on the street or in the store after tampering with our toys.

What has made customers so vain? How did "customerization" make its way into the DNA of service? The reasons are complex. As organizations shifted us away from generalist toward specialist they created a two-headed monster. Specialists are both better-equipped and accustomed to tailor-making our experience. Even manufacturers can put our predilections in the production concoction to yield outcomes and outputs we prefer. We get used to the made-to-order feature of service. We like hotels that remember we like a hard pillow, bartenders that recall our special drink, and hair stylists that remember we prefer they go easy on the hairspray. And we avoid those who cannot, or do not.

But, this specialization has also created distance, tacitly shifting the customer from participant to observer. The energy of the encounter is devoted to displaying expertise, not fostering customer inclusion. Next time you go to a store exclusively devoted to shoes, electronics, coffee, cars, or ice cream, notice how much attention is given to you and your requirements versus their product and its features. Compare the bravado of know-how with the compassion of customer partnership.

Customers start young wanting everything their way. A teddy bear is now a Build-a-Bear workshop. The perennial Barbie doll has become accessorize-Barbie online. Even American Girl dolls now come with matching outfits for "mommy." Want to decorate your new cell phone? There is a huge after-market industry enabling customization, from desktop stands to protective covers to ringtones. Customers flock to sites like StumbleUpon.com to view only websites tailored to their preferences. Dell Computer built a powerful business on letting customers customize their computers. The filtering capacity of prominent one-to-one companies has made unwanted computer spam even more of an irritant than the proliferation of junk mail customers once tolerated.

One of the hottest entries in the personalization world is an advanced analytics program called RAMP (Real-Time Analytics Matching Platform). It enables an inbound call to be matched with the best customer rep in real time. "It's the eHarmony of business call centers," said Cameron Hurst, a VP with Assurant and user of RAMP. According to Kate Leggett, senior analyst for customer service at Forrester Research, "RAMP not only matches agents to callers based on a set of attributes . . . but is intelligent enough to select the agent best suited to handle a caller irrespective of whether the agent is currently available or not."[7] "It's the sweet spot," said Toby Cook of IBM Global Business Services. "We find that people are willing to wait longer if they get the best person."[8]

"Personalization is the killer app for business rules," says Ronald Ross, co-founder of Business Rule Solutions. Business rules are the instructions that inform computers (and people) how to operate consistently.[9] Research demonstrates most customers prefer personalization. Personalization has been shown to significantly increase click-through rates.[10] Another research study found that a content-targeting approach increased click-throughs by 62 percent.[11] Personalizing copy in a book offer significantly increased response rates.[12]

Valuing the Vain

The etymology of words can often be very instructive. Vain, as we have used it in this chapter, means "overly concerned with oneself." It is the part of us all that wants events to go our way, things to revolve around our needs, and experiences to be crafted to reflect our preferences.

However, vain also means "empty." Too much "plain vanilla" leaves us bored and drab. Customers are drawn to the carnival side of Whole Foods Markets, Stew Leonard's Dairy, and Trader Joe's because they have a stimulating—some might say titillating—quality that awakens the spirit. Hotel Monaco turns an all-too-predictable hotel stay into a special treat by providing zebra-patterned bathrobes instead of hospital white, an unexpected surprise on the pillow at turndown instead of the proverbial mint, and a goldfish to keep a guest company. But the most powerful antidote to "empty" is creating a service experience that is personalized and generous.

Go to

Customers enjoy service that is "all about them." It requires adding more sizzle to the experience. It might include personalizing the experience. Tool #8 provides tips for serving as an expert. Tool #13 provides an array of ways to add an element of delight or pleasant surprise.

Our friend Shaun Smith, of Smith+co in London, shared with us his favorite Lexus story as an example. A BMW owner walked into a Lexus dealership and announced that he was considering changing automobile brands. He had seen an ad about Lexus's legendary service. But first he had a service question for the Lexus salesperson.

"Earlier this week I took my BMW in for routine maintenance. In the process they removed the ashtray to clean it but forgot to put it back. When I discovered it was missing, I called the BMW service manager. He said they had indeed found the wayward ashtray shortly after I left and would be happy to hold it up front in the office for me to pick up at my convenience. Now, how would you have handled this situation?"

The Lexus salesperson replied, "Well, sir, it would not have happened since we have a 54-item checklist that includes replacing the ashtray after cleaning. But, if it were to have happened, we would not have waited for you to call us."

The BMW owner smiled and left the showroom.

That afternoon after work, the Lexus salesperson drove to the BMW dealership, picked up the customer's ashtray, and surprised him with it at the front door of his home!

PART TWO

The Resolution
Manifesto: The Wired and Dangerous Link

> When I took office, only high energy physicists had
> ever heard of what is called the worldwide web . . .
> now even my cat has its own page.
>
> Former President Bill Clinton

What do the Sears Roebuck catalog and the birth control pill have in common? Both revolutionized the experience of the recipient.

In the late 1800s Americans moved west following the emergence and expansion of the railroads. When the postal system was added near the turn of the century, it created the conditions for the birth of the mail-order catalog. Richard Sears, always a genius with clever phrases, bannered the cover of the first Sears Roebuck catalog with "Book of Bargains: A Money Saver for Everyone," "Cheapest Supply House on Earth," and "Our trade reaches around the World."

The Sears Roebuck catalog gave farmers in rural areas and pioneers in remote settlements access to a wide array of products otherwise unavailable within hundreds of miles. The catalog included watches, sewing machines, sporting goods, musical instruments, saddles, firearms, buggies, bicycles, baby carriages, and clothing. The 1895 catalog added eyeglasses, along with a self-administered eye test for "old sight, near sight, and astigmatism." Miners in the mountains of Utah were able to buy complete houses shipped west on a train. "Your money back if you are not satisfied" was added to catalogs in 1903, complete with Richard Sears's handwritten note to his customers.[1]

And the birth control pill? Letty Cottin Pogrebin, the founding editor of *Ms. Magazine* and author of nine books, told of the birth and power of the pill in an interview for CNN Opinion:

> In 1962, when I was a 22-year-old Holly Golightly-wannabe living in Greenwich Village with my dog and my motor scooter, an event had a seismic effect on my life. . . . My doctor at the time wrote me a prescription for The Pill. . . . The impact of The Pill was radical. It meant sex need not lead to pregnancy. But it wasn't just another form of contraception, it was an equalizer, a liberator, and easy to take. For the first time in human history, a woman could control her sexuality and determine her readiness for reproduction by swallowing a pill smaller than an aspirin. Critics warned that The Pill would spawn generations of loose, immoral women; what it spawned was generations of empowered women who are better equipped to make rational choices about their lives.[2]

Combine the reach and access of the Sears Roebuck catalog to pioneers in far-flung rural areas with the empowering impact on women of The Pill and you have something like the effect of the Internet on today's customers. Add power to access and you have the means to put capacity and competence in the hands of customers. But, there is a double edge here. Just as the syringe that delivers life-saving medicine to a patient can also shoot mind-numbing heroin into an addict, the Internet has been as potentially intimidating as it has been potentially enlightening. Its effect on customers has taken many forms.

Wired Is a Means to Connect

Imagine how different the outcome of the American Revolution would have been if Paul Revere had elected to leave his horse in the barn and simply write a letter to the mayor of every small town between Lexington and Concord advising them "The British are coming!" Too many organizations are sending out letters to customers instead of riding the horse of instant connection. Author and consultant Pete Blackshaw has named this phenomenon "consumer-generated media, or CGM." He defines consumer-generated media as "the currency of a new commercial relationship between business and consumers. It is the endless stream of comments, opinions, emotions, and personal stories about any and every company, product, service, or brand which consumers can now post online and broadcast to millions of other consumers with the click of a mouse."[3]

Wired Is a Tool to Accelerate

Customers' concept of time has dramatically changed. Few people today delay reviewing their emails until they can get home or to the office to fire up a computer. Text messaging has replaced dialing; fax machines are viewed as obsolete. More important, the customer's sense of urgency has forced organizational life to become 24/7. For customers, an organization that closes its merchandizing access at 5 p.m. is a bit like Paul Revere electing to wait until morning instead of mounting his steed at midnight.

Like it or not, it means every enterprise on the planet must reconceptualize its habits and practices regarding time and speed. It necessitates creating easy access when customers want it; it means providing a supersonic response that matches the customer's "I want it now" attention span.

Wired Is a Resource to Instruct

Ask people in most organizations about how they get customer feedback and you will get a sermonette on their scientifically sanitized customer survey. The higher-ups would rather wait for J.D. Power results than visit the factory floor, ride in the truck with a service tech, or sit in the call center listening to customer calls. Real time feedback is too often viewed as complaint management by the frontline, not as a powerful source of customer insight and postmortem forensics. Monitoring social media as a means of instant learning and rapid intervention is far from mainstream. Meanwhile, edgy customers vilify to the digital masses a service hiccup in the evening and by morning the organization is surprised by the arrival of "the British."

Author Pete Blackshaw relates the story of what Comcast faced in 2006:

> . . . Comcast found itself in the middle of a viral firestorm when a guy named Brian Finklestein found a Comcast technician asleep on his couch. Making matters worse, the technician had fallen asleep waiting for Comcast's own customer support line to answer the phone. Finkelstein quickly took a video of the sleeping repairman and posted it to YouTube, where it was viewed by a half-million people within hours. The story was, of course, picked up by bloggers, MSNBC, and several national newspapers; it continues to punish Comcast by showing up in search results."[4]

Wired Is a Forum to Unite

When we were kids, one of the coolest communications with buddies was constructing a "phone line" using a long string with an empty bean can on either end. When you spoke right into the bean can, the sound carried over the string to be heard by the ear in the can on the other end. We could trade secrets and tell racy jokes without parental eavesdropping. We even figured out a way to connect several cans creating our own "crowdalogue." It became the best way to plan pranks on younger siblings or kids we didn't like.

The Internet has features similar to the party-line bean cans on a string. When one person tells another person in an email about an experience at Acme Pyrotechnics, it is the computer version of word of mouth. But, when customers access their entire buddy list of 850 friends instantly and most of their friends follow suit, contacting their own buddy lists, they can create a hero or horror overnight. Their virtually instant communications can have the power and punch of business insurrection, creating a candidate for bankruptcy by the end of the week. And, given the degree customers "listen" and value the reviews of other customers, their influence can spread like a pandemic, with devastating impact on the bottom line of the victim in the cross-hairs of one computer mouse.

Wired Is the Great Equalizer

One of the most curious pieces of demagoguery coming out of the 2007–2009 recession was the drama pitting "Wall Street" against "Main Street." Wall Streeters were positioned as gluttonous, evil mon-eychangers against whom the tables should be turned by the common people of Main Street who were victims of their wily ways. The fact is there is no Wall Street without Main Street, and vice versa. The Internet has been a tool for egalitarianism. David has exactly the same arsenal as Goliath. The advent of social media has kept cyberspace operating with norms similar to those of a small town.

Tara Hunt, in her ground-breaking book *The Whuffie Factor,* referred to the new norms of social media as whuffie, a term coined by Cory Doctorow. "Whuffie," Hunt wrote, "is the residual outcome—the currency—of your reputation. You lose or gain it based on positive and negative actions, your contribution to the community. . . ." Influence comes through "being nice, being networked, and being notable." "There is no room for bullies with lots of money. Money may buy you an audience but it will not guarantee influence."[5]

In January 2008, *The Economist* published an article reporting a fascinating alteration in customer behavior.

> In 2006 EMI, the fourth-biggest recorded music company in the world, invited some teenagers into its headquarters in London to talk to its top managers about their listening habits. At the end of the session the EMI bosses thanked them for their comments and told them to help themselves to a big pile of CDs

sitting on a table. But none of the teens took any of the CDs, even though they were free. "That was the moment we realized the game was completely up," says a person who was there.[6]

Why the Mouse Is Roaring

The Service Museum would likely have a special display on the infamous Word of Mouth. It has been the historical means by which customers learned about great service and lousy service beyond their own experience. Sure, they could read the PR drivel and advertising claims the company crafted, but that transmission was suspect to all but the most gullible and uninformed. We kinda sorta trusted the brand spokespersons—fictitious ones like Betty Crocker, Aunt Jemima, and Mr. Clean, as well as real ones like Michael Jordan, George Foreman, and Florence Henderson. And, there were also the surrogate judges—the Good Housekeeping Seal, the Better Business Bureau, and J.D. Power—that gave us some degree of assurance. But, the most trusted source was what Larry next door had to say.

The computer mouse changed all that. Word of Mouse has replaced word of mouth as the most viral means of gossip, grousing and groaning about last night's slow restaurant service, yesterday's rude sales clerk, or this morning's glitch on Acme.com. As was earlier noted, today's Internet connections, whether blogs, tweets, or other forms of social media, have five times the impact of traditional word of mouth.[7]

The change in the service covenant has altered the social outlet that service historically has provided. When Duke Energy closed 99 local payment centers to consolidate to a single centralized call center, the complaint was not about the quality of service. According to then VP of Customer Service, Sharon Decker, it was about the nature of service. Instead of talking with the neighbor at the Duke Office downtown, the customer was now talking with a stranger. While the stranger could deal with the request much faster, more knowledgeably, and around the clock, it was not the Tammy or Todd the customer knew from church. And that was almost twenty years ago!

With customers cut off from the customary social connection that has been the cornerstone of commerce, the Internet has become the surrogate. The more service delivery becomes impersonal, the more the customer turns to the Internet as the conduit to commercial conversation. There are pockets of customers called cocooners who, thanks to the Internet and UPS, are able to engage in all their buying activity without ever having to leave their nest.

The difference between the village of yesteryear and the cybervillage of today is the fact that customers create their own village. Residents of the old-timey village were typically there due to the accident of their birth or relocation. Now, the customer can vote you in or out of their Facebook, Linkedin, or MySpace city limits. And since all in my village are my choice, when I register a concern, they are far more likely to echo my sentiment to all those in their village!

The Revenge of the Mouse

Dell Computer ran headfirst into the power of the Internet-enabled customer a few years ago. As chronicled in Kim Williams's case study, "Dell Hell: The Impact of Social Media on Corporate Communication," in June 2005 Dell Inc. received some major complaints concerning its customer support services. One of these complaints was from Jeff Jarvis, an Internet blogger.

Soon after Jeff purchased a new Dell laptop, it malfunctioned. After contacting Dell's customer support, Jeff was told he would need to send the machine back to the company because the technician would not be able to come to his home with the parts he would need (Jeff had purchased a four-year warranty with home support). This exchange upset Jeff and he began to vent his frustrations about his experience on his blog at Buzzmachine.com in a series of posts, nicknamed "Dell Hell."

When he received his computer back it still did not work. Jeff sent a string of emails to Dell customer service and continued to tell his story via his blog. He received a number of email responses from

Dell with the wrong customer name and decided that no one at Dell was listening. The only way he was able to elicit action from Dell was to write the executive in charge of Dell's U.S. consumer business. He was offered a total refund, which he accepted. He used it to purchase an Apple.[8]

Meanwhile thousands of disgruntled Dell customers posted comments or linked to Jeff's blog. The activity attracted media attention and was soon reported by Computerworld and Intelliseek, among others. Michigan University's American Customer Satisfaction Index (ACSI) showed Dell's customer service rating had dropped 5 points in a year.[9] This is significant because ACSI has documented a strong relationship between ACSI score and both market share and stock price. ACSI scores and the companies' share prices historically tend to move in the same direction. ACSI's research has found the range of that stock price drop averaged between 1 percent to 5 percent based upon the industry for each respective business.[10]

"Desperadoes Waiting for a Train"

"Desperadoes Waiting for a Train" is a song made famous by the Highwaymen, a singing group made up of country music giants Kris Kristofferson, Willie Nelson, and the late Waylon Jennings and Johnny Cash. It perfectly captures the sense of eagerness customers have today. Unlike the patient, willing-to-wait customers of yesteryear, customers today want instant everything. They can't wait for a fax anymore. And, overnighting anything seems like an eternity. Precious documents are scanned and emailed, rarely mailed. Sending something via the postal service now is called "snail mail." Got a document too large to send, we use warehouses in cyberspace (like YouSendIt.com and 4Shared.com) to avoid bringing pain to our servers.

To say customers are wired not only means they are Internet-connected but it also implies the edginess brought on by superfast availability in a 24/7 world. Wired means "hyper" or "restless," as well as "bound together." Zappos.com made the record books and "Best of" lists, not because of the quality of its merchandise or the zippiness of its website, but due to its ability to get you merchandise way before you expected it. Order a pair of shoes on your home computer after supper, and they are on your doorstep the next morning—and you are not charged a dime for the jet plane ride that brought them there. It is a service experience that perfectly fits the restlessness of today's customer.

We have littered this book with the language of upheaval. We see it in our clients; we experience it in our personal and professional lives. The transformation of the service covenant, the alteration of the character of the customer, and the potent quality of the Internet have made the world of commerce like a bomb waiting for someone to light the fuse. On the entertainment front, the Internet turned a $25,000 film called *The Blair Witch Project* into a $250 million megahit. On the political front, some claim Obama's edge in the 2008 U.S. presidential election was largely due to his campaign's savvy use of the Internet, both for reaching his base and raising contributions. Social media played a significant role in bringing down the dictatorial governments of Tunisia and Egypt in early 2011. The Internet will likely foster the creation of a formidable national third party within the next decade.

The solution is not to "just get rid of the Internet." The Internet is here to stay. The edginess present in many customers was not caused by the Internet. One could make a case that their picky nature has been the result of the pain of the last recession. The vocal nature of customers has been increasing ever since companies began actively to seek feedback. That was not an Internet-driven change. And, the pursuit of "all about me" service has been fueled by the capacity of organizations to offer customers more diversity than "one size fits all."

The solution lies in renewing the service covenant. Customers enjoy the efficiency of self-serve; they do not enjoy being excluded or abandoned. Customers react negatively to "I don't think there's anybody back there" (as actress Clara Peller said in the famous Wendy's ad). Customers value the time savings of service automation. They do not want automation that makes them believe they are devalued, isolated, and excluded. Customers gain from the deep knowledge of a specialist, but emotional distance between teacher and pupil reminds them unpleasantly of their dependence.

The new service covenant can turn turbulence into calm and restlessness into tranquility only to the degree it infuses customer transactions and relationships with the feeling of partnership. It will require service providers' rethinking how service is designed and delivered. It will take repositioning the customers, not as cash machines or consumers, but as the experience co-creators they really are. The cost for continuing on the same familiar path is not just the loss of one customer, or two, or ten. The price tag will be the arson of a reputation fueled by a dangerous customer armed with a "lighted mouse."

CHAPTER 6

How the Service Covenant Can Be Rebalanced

"There is absolutely no ambiguity about the true meaning of a back blast," barked the Army sergeant as he cautioned recruits in boot camp to avoid getting behind an anti-tank bazooka (now the M72 LAW) about to be fired. How many things in life have "absolutely no ambiguity about their true meaning"?

It got us thinking about the true meaning of "customer service." If the restaurant has salt and pepper on your table, is that customer service? What if they gave you an air-conditioned room in which to dine in the summer? Would you call the elevator in the office building customer service? How about the ATM machine?

Some might say yes to all. They would broad-stroke it all, from condiments on the table to the concierge in a five-star hotel. But, that covers a lot of ground. It not only waters down the concept to be practically meaningless, it leaves a lot of room for ambiguity. This vagueness contributes to leaders' believing their customer service is good when their customers think it is poor.

A Hierarchy of Service

One of the best definitions of customer service we know was posited by writer Jamier Scott: "Customer service is a series of activities designed to enhance the level of customer satisfaction—that is, the feel-

Figure 1. Customer Service Loyalty

ing that a product or service has met the customer expectation."[1] But, even Mr. Scott broad-strokes the meaning with his "activities" label. What if we put customer service on a continuum or on a hierarchy, much like Abraham Maslow did in his attempt to explain human motivation? After all, is there not a similarity between worker motivation and customer affinity?

When people ask questions like "Is self-service better than full-service?" it implies either-or thinking that may be missing the point—like asking a senior citizen in a nursing home which is better, a back rub or a visit from the family. Thinking of customer service more as a progression or hierarchy captures the true meaning of customer service (see Figure 1).

End result is the basic level of customer service; it involves simply getting the desired effect or outcome. We often refer to this level as service "air"—since, just like the air we breathe, we take it for granted unless it is absent or threatened. An airline passenger expects the plane to land safely in the right city on time with luggage in tow. End result is the given or table stake of customer service. Much like Maslow's basic or survival level on his needs hierarchy, if your physiological needs are unmet, nothing else matters.

Ease is the next level in service motivation. As customers, we expect service to be without hassle. We require it to be rendered with limited effort on our part. The more energy we have to exert to get basic service requirements met, the lower the assessment of the experience. As service-seeking customers, we do not like bureaucracy; we resent wait, forms, rigid rules—any service requirement that has us jump through hoops. Self-service, done well, makes getting service easier, faster, and simpler.

Engagement is the service version of Maslow's social or belonging need. As social people we value service providers who host, support, and collaborate with us to ensure we get what we need, want, and expect. We enjoy service providers who are friendly, knowledgeable, and helpful. We prefer a connection that acknowledges us as a person, not a number, consumer, or "next in line." We value those who show us courtesy and respect. The journey through service land is much more caring and encouraging when we have a guide and champion to go with us, or at least to ensure our journey is a pleasant one.

Extra reminds us that we are special and important to the service provider. It is the service level that puts a cherry on top of the experience. The pinnacle of extra is when the service experience is tailor-made for a particular customer. As customers, we enjoy service "our way." When a service provider goes the extra mile to provide value-added, it communicates that we are valued and important. Extra is the realm of delight, not just satisfaction. It is the kind of experience that creates a special surprise that yields a story to tell and reason to return. It turns retention into loyalty.

Exhilaration is as rare in service as self-actualization is in Maslow's motivation peak in people. It is a service experience that surfaces the best of who we are as people. It is enriching and ennobling. Often laced with generosity, it is the specialty of the service provider that epitomizes the very essence of what it means "to serve." Bill Marriott likes to refer to this kind of service as the nobility of service—designed to touch your soul and reawaken your spirit. Think of exhilaration as service from providers who view serving as a calling with a quest of ensuring the recipients of their efforts are moved by the experience.

Operationalizing the Service Hierarchy

Social psychology pioneer Kurt Lewin wrote, "There is nothing so practical as a good theory." However, theories on paper offer little more than intellectual entertainment and academic speculation. Practicality can only result when the theory instructs us in ways that enhance or improve practice.

What can the service hierarchy tell us? First, it suggests that service is multifaceted. If a customer wants a cold can of soda and nothing more, a convenient vending machine that keeps its promise is probably sufficient. However, that same soda with a gourmet meal for a special-occasion dining experience might require delivery by an elegant waiter. In other words, the manner the customer defines service adequacy varies with time, place, and circumstance.

Service wisdom comes with knowing the requirements and expectations of the target customer and possessing the flexibility to shift when the context changes what the customer desires. A business hotel on Tuesday can become a destination hotel on the weekend. Even if the same customer visits mid-week and on the weekend, the Tuesday service-on-the-run business traveler will likely demand a more pampering experience on Saturday, especially if sharing it with a special person.

The service hierarchy also tells us that the higher the level on the hierarchy, the greater the propensity for loyalty. Getting a fundamental service need met with minimal or zero effort is not the stuff of customer devotion. We all enjoy the comfort of knowing the lights will come on when we flip the wall switch, but no one races to the phone or computer to tell a friend about the greatness of plain vanilla electric service. The first two levels on the hierarchy are likely to be only the realm for satisfaction, not loyalty . . . and, certainly not for ardent advocacy.

Loyalty, therefore, begins at engagement—that part of the hierarchy where people as servers (not machines) reside. Even if partially automated, it is the realm where the guardian of the service covenant lives and remains obviously vigilant over the service encounter. When things go wrong, solutions to resolving disappointment cannot come from the **End Result** or **Ease** level of the hierarchy, but must come from the **Engagement** level or above. **Extra** is engagement done with excellence and generosity; **Exhilaration** is engagement done with character and soul.

Customers as Partners

Now, for the most important lesson of the service hierarchy. The purest form of engagement—the one best at restoring the service covenant—is a partnership.

Let's return to our premise. Whether the Internet was the cause or simply the enabler of customers' newfound supremacy is irrelevant. The fact is that today's customers, edgy from all that has transpired, now rule! This has produced anxiety, apprehension and worry on both sides of the service covenant. The path to service tranquility—peace between server and served—is the restoration and renewal of the service covenant.

Partnership is the model we have selected as the restorative foundation of the renewed service covenant. Partnership, in its purest form, is a reflection of egalitarianism—collaboration and cooperation sourced from a commitment to transparency, authenticity, and mutuality. When customers feel like partners—true partners—they not only experience more commitment and ownership (since they are serving *with*)—but they also make the service provider a part of their village. When service providers act like partners, they demonstrate assertive inclusion, dramatic listening, genuine openness and a deep allegiance to fairness and generosity.

A solid partnership reflects a collection of principles, protocols, and practices that govern and ground how equals co-labor together on one another's behalf. Done well, they ensure vigor will remain in the union; properly maintained, they guarantee values will aid the alliance in withstanding adversity and maintaining perseverance in times of challenge.

Partners take care of each other. When partners make mistakes, they are quick to own the error, agile in correcting it, and driven to rebalance the relationship as they mend the mistake. Partners do not lie or deceive. Partners will not act out of greed or self-indulgence. Most important, partners never take their valued relationship for granted.

The byproduct of a partnership approach to the service covenant is its attraction to apprehensive customers as a place of tranquility. The outcome of partnership is the return of soul to service. It is the purest manifestation of a confederation laced in balance and harmony.

Partnership Principles in Action

What follows is the partnership framework key to ensuring a solid, trust-producing service covenant. It includes grounding (managing self), connection (managing the customer experience) and congruence (managing the service setting). To these three we have added a fourth component, acumen, that, through its renewal and learning function, makes the other three succeed (see Figure 2).

Grounding

Grounding is the pursuit of internal tranquility. We all enjoy being served by a person who demonstrates confidence laced with warmth. A pleasant professional who can get things done on our behalf helps allay our reservations regarding whether we will get a return on our investment of time and funds. People who show such command presence are typically at peace (or at least peace *enough*) to freely communicate an authentic spirit of service. The engine of their service tranquility is a sense of purpose or mission. If service were a religion, their locomotion would be labeled a calling. The energy of their service tranquility is a

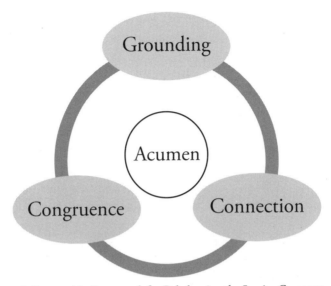

Figure 2. Partnership Framework for Rebalancing the Service Covenant

passion for service—an inner drive to bring their best to the encounter. This energy reflects an attitude we will call "the spirit of greatness." Its contagious nature alters the balance between the server and the served, spreading important tranquility to the relationship.

Connection

Connection is the manifestation of interpersonal tranquility—service provider to customer. It is a key tenet of the new service covenant. The old understanding between service customer and provider displayed little suspicion, caution, or reserve. It was a feature of a time when both believed the other would be honest—and they always were. It was an era when customer and service provider trusted that differences would be resolved with a sense of fair play—and they typically were.

Today, customers enter the service encounter with antennae raised high, surveying the scene for the impending possibility of disappointment. Service providers are likewise on guard, skittish about the potential of a litigious aftermath and worried that a minor misstep will be broadcast on the marquee of tonight's Facebook status update or post. It is a recipe for rigidity and concern. Bringing apparent equilibrium to an otherwise out-of-balance scene can surface tranquility and ensure triumph.

Since the centerpiece of this book is the customer, you will discover later in the book that we have expanded the basic Connection concept (Chapter 8) to encompass two particularly challenging types—Bad Connections (Chapter 9) and Wired Connections (Chapter 10). Bad connections are those occasions when the customer is more than simply anxious or apprehensive; they are upset, angry, or furious because of a service failure that has left them feeling extremely disappointed or victimized. Wired Connections include the special challenge of dealing with customers on the Internet, devoid of the verbals and non-verbals that contribute to understanding and trust. We separated the two challenging types into their own chapters because we have learned through our work with clients that, while the overarching partnership philosophy fits both, the practical application is unique to the circumstance.

Congruence

Congruence is the assurance of serenity in all the inanimate components of the service encounter—the props of the service performance. When processes work to benefit the server but not the served, there is an imbalance in the covenant. If the tools, aids, forms, codes, and setting in any way fail to support the covenant, they contribute to tension, albeit subtly and often subconsciously.

Congruence comes when there is a deliberate and successful effort to bring trust and confidence to the customer while also contributing to the comfort of the service provider. If either side of the service equation is inappropriately inconvenienced or treated without consideration, the board "tilts" and the service game ends, even if it is not yet over. Congruence is the demonstration of reliability when consistency bolsters trust. It is the expression of scenography when the aesthetics of the service encounter are at play.

Acumen

Acumen is the preservation of past and future competence. It entails the perpetual pursuit of customer intelligence as well as the thoughtful customer forensics that can come from postmortems and historical analyses. Its power lies in its capacity to help self-regulate so that tranquility can be maintained. Its force comes from its capability to bring confidence to service providers, enabling a proactive response to an otherwise cautious customer. Acumen has much in common with the preparation side of confident speech-making, turning stage fright into charisma. It is more than the pursuit of information. It also means an attitude of curiosity, combining the humility to learn with the evergreen means of remaining astute.

/\/\/\/

There is an important line in the movie *National Treasure*.* Patrick Gates (played by Jon Voight) cautions his son Ben (played by Nicolas Cage), at a moment of peril when they were being held captive by the bad guys: "Cooperation only lasts as long as the status quo is unchanged. As soon as this guy gets to wherever this thing ends, he won't need you any more, or—or any of us." Gates's reference to status quo was not about resisting change; it was about maintaining balance.

Cooperation with self, customers, and the setting happens when the status quo is achieved and kept constant. At one end of the balance is the treasure of a service provider filled with the pride of knowing a difference was made in the life of another. At the other end is a customer delighted with the experience of worth being exchanged in a fashion that reaffirmed a belief in the goodness of mankind.

---

*National Treasure was a 2004 movie produced by Walt Disney Productions and based on a story by Jim Kouf, Oren Aviv, and Charles Segars.

CHAPTER 7

Grounding

How to Balance Yourself for Partnership

You can tell you are about to meet a carrier of balance and tranquility when a colleague's face lights up as he announces "Let me get David for you." The coworker's animated look lodges your eager anticipation somewhere between "You're in for a treat" and "You ain't gonna believe this!"

Then it happens. You come to face to face with a person who has fallen hopelessly in love with his role!

We were staying at the Marriott Oak Brook near Chicago and were having drinks with a client before going on to a nearby restaurant to meet another client for dinner. Running a bit behind schedule, we were anxious about making our dinner reservation in time. The restaurant was beyond walking distance but an insultingly short haul for a taxi driver. Fortunately, the hotel van was available and bell stand attendant David Harris could transport us. Rather than abandoning our half-finished drinks, we had elected to take them with us, especially since David was to be our designated driver.

Now imagine this. You can "feel" David emotionally long before he shakes your hand. His enthusiasm is so apparent that his style and spirit meet you before he does. The first thing you notice is David's glowing Steinway smile—like he just unexpectedly encountered two long-lost boyhood friends. The second thing you notice is his gait; it reveals a man extremely eager to connect and raring to serve. Finally, you witness how his gusto infects every single soul within earshot with a robust case of the grins.

"Is it true I get the grand pleasure of being the chauffeur for you gentlemen tonight?" he asks in a tone like he was still pinching himself after winning a big prize! We felt like members of an exclusive club as we boarded his chariot of joy. His style allayed our worries about getting to the restaurant on time.

"You gentlemen don't spill your grape juice," David teased as he made a sharp corner just shy of the restaurant. It was obvious he was crystal clear on the contents of our adult-beverage cups and was having a blast accommodating our slight departure from customary van rules.

Depositing us at the restaurant he gave us each a two-handed shake and his business card. "Would you gentlemen please call me when you finish dinner? I can be here in five minutes! And, if you want to bring back a few buddies for a nightcap, we would love to take care of them as well." We literally wanted to rush through dinner just to hurry and get a return visit from the joyful spirit of David Harris![1]

The Anatomy of the Balance Carrier

Customer tranquility starts with service provider serenity. David was a source of solace for us because of his focused, generous, and joyful manner. He gave the impression that the role he held was what he had always wanted to be when he grew up, even though we suspected working the bell stand was really just a step on his path to higher status. He was the personification of a man at peace, someone creating a place of pleasure with his own wit, will, and wherewithal. Our memorable experience was handmade by a person who was operating from a solid grounding of bigheartedness and a spirit of greatness. If positive attitude was looking for a poster child, David could have been the model. He was a carrier of tranquility, infecting all around him.

Balance carriers like David are easy to spot. First and foremost, they are focused and seemingly incapable of being distracted. With such a focus on the customer, you cannot help but feel valued. They parade charisma without "charging admission." When a politician shows you charisma, you put your hand on your wallet. When actors display charisma, you get your money's worth. But the charm of a carrier of balance is just there for you to enjoy—no strings are attached.

Balance carriers seem liberated from the ties that bind most of us. They are not easily derailed or bothered by edgy customers who have been turned bitter or cynical by their experiences on the planet. Their freedom is not an expression of rebellion or revolt. They show their joyful spirit because that is who they are, not because they have anything to prove. They seem to source a sense of purpose that is energized by a passion to serve.

What is it about this special breed of service provider that turns them into Pied Pipers of sorts, making customers want to fall in line behind them in hopes that some of the joyful spirit might rub off? How do they create such service calm in a milieu of mayhem and an atmosphere of anxiety? David Harris provides us a ready-made specimen to dissect, explore, and understand.

David Was Focused

The morning after our "freedom ride" with David we reflected on the special experience. What had made it so inviting and refreshing? What was it about David that caused us to feel so peaceful about sharing the adventure with him? Was this a serendipitous moment or was this the everyday David? Was this nature, nurture, or the handiwork of some superior leader? If we could open up this internal tranquility-making machine, what would we find inside?

It was abundantly clear that David was focused on us and performing his role on our behalf as well as his. He was like a craftsman enamored with his trade and amazed at how it impacted others. He was not a performer in pursuit of applause or a server eager to win a gratuity. He was just focused on enjoying his role for the pure, simple pleasure it brought to both served and server. David obviously enjoyed the effect he was having. Yet it was clear he likely would have had a great time just "playing by himself."

Customers today do not enter the service encounter with the expectation of an inspired experience. Unless they are visiting an amusement park, are friends with the owner, or enjoying a five-star restaurant, they anticipate a relatively humdrum, functional experience. Let's call that position neutral. However, many customers bring with them service baggage from prior experiences that put them on alert that the acceptable might become gloomy. That means they are actually in a negative position from the get-go. So the service provider must deliver a better-than-expected experience in order to get expectations at least back to neutral. If the service provider delivers an apathetic performance, the customer service barometer remains in the negative zone. Since the non-animate parts of the service encounter have no feelings, it makes the human server a vital piece of the "balancing" act.

As customers enter a service experience, their path to tranquility begins with the experience that they are valued. When a service provider puts the laser beam of undivided attention on them, it signals to the customer that they are the centerpiece, not the service provider's task or chore. David was serving us, not just doing his job. And, we were convinced of that stance by his keen interest, intense curiosity, and refusal to be distracted by anything else around him.

He seemed to want to bring his best to the experience. As humans we are attracted to those experiences that connect with our best side. Human interest stories tug at our heart; we pull for the underdog in our innate quest for "the right thing." We are awed by Olympic champions, inspired by pioneers, and touched when we lose a great leader, performer, or hero. Yet, there are too few incidents that take our breath away with the same amazement as a gorgeous sunset, outstanding athletic feat, or brilliant magic trick. The dissonance produced by traffic, spam, clutter, and canned laughter numbs our spirits and monotonizes our routines. It makes focused and purposeful service presentations especially compelling.

David Was Focused on Giving

What is the act of service, really? As customers, we associate it with assistance or help—doing a good deed that benefits another. However, for such a benefit to matter it must fall outside the realm of routine. When we get our car repaired we bring with our vehicle certain expectations. We expect the work to be done accurately and with limited wait. We expect the mechanic to "clean up afterwards"—no grease on our car seat. We also expect when we retrieve our repaired vehicle to have to get out our wallet. We only recall such a standard encounter if the experience exceeds or fails to meet our expectations.

Enhancing the worth of the server-to-customer exchange—value-added or value-unique—comes from an internal spirit of generosity. If the auto mechanic takes the time to explain the repair in a way that helps prevent a future occurrence, if the service writer leaves an ice-cold bottle of water in the car cup holder, or if the repair bill notes another problem was corrected without charge, we would describe that repair-for-money exchange as "great service" and tell our neighbors. We are moved and made to feel more peaceful by that kind of generosity.

Customer tranquility comes when service enriches the exchange. Customers feel valued when the service provider delivers something special to the encounter. But generosity must be coupled with conscientiousness or it turns contentment into caution. A generous heart without an enthusiastic spirit risks leaving customers believing they have received a mere gesture or witnessed a simple ploy. The soul of service generosity is hospitality.

The two of us were en route to a meeting and stopped for lunch. We are major fans of McDonald's french fries—the best in the world. We also enjoy the Chick-fil-A salads. Luckily the two fast-food restaurants were right next door to each other.

We parked between the two and walked first into Mickey D's for the fries. The place was like a human vending machine—fast and functional. But, the Chick-fil-A experience was completely different! We could feel the upbeat warmth as soon as we opened their door. The counter person smiled and greeted us with "Thank you for being our guests! What can I tempt you with today?" Every employee had the same hosting spirit.

As we were leaving, we asked an employee, "How come this is so different than over there?" We pointed at the Golden Arches. "Oh," she said with a grin, "over there, they serve customers, but here we are hosts to our guests." Spotting our foreign fries, she continued: "Over there you just get the fries. But, here we give you a great experience. You may not remember those fries tomorrow; but we hope you will remember your visit with us, even if you forget what you ordered."

Service with soul is about serving unconditionally. It means losing yourself in the interest of the customer. It is service emanating from the inner joy of service, not a tactical decision. And, its magical power for creating balance and tranquility works only when there is no requirement or expectation of a response in kind. It is an endowment made out of a heartfelt urge to contribute.

David Was Focused on Spreading Joy

Watching David in action you get the distinct impression that his mother forgot to tell him to be quiet. He likely was encouraged to laugh as loud as he wanted to, which enabled him to grow up without a built-in governor on his delight meter. He no doubt developed a comfort and confidence for expressing joy beyond the boundaries of most people.

An unbridled joyful style like David's has a captivating power on customers. Being in the presence of David-like employees makes customers feel as Melvin (played by Jack Nicholson) must have been feeling in the movie *As Good As It Gets** when he told new girlfriend Carol (played by Helen Hunt), "You make me want to be a better man!" It's difficult to misbehave or stay cranky in the company of such a joy giver. Few among us want to drag storm clouds into the perpetually sunny skies of such life forms.

---

* *As Good As It Gets* is a 1997 film directed by James Brooks and based on the story by Mark Andrus.

Several weeks after our joy ride with David we encountered him again on a return visit to the hotel. We were waiting for a colleague to join us in the lobby when David walked through the area. His exuberance was just as infectious as we remembered. "You gentlemen going to be here for several days?" he asked, as if he'd been asking a boyhood friend's mom, "Can Johnny come out and play?"

Sensing we had time to kill, David turned up the volume on his happiness-giving curiosity. His questions were clearly constructed from sincere interest: he wanted nothing more than to understand us. We found ourselves telling him more than we would normally share with a virtual stranger. Carriers of tranquility are like that—their complete absence of judgment invites unexplained openness and unexpected candor. Because they come from a place that is unguarded and genuine, they invite the same attitude and response from others.

Joyful servers also are notable for their never-say-die resilience, boldly standing up when others around them are timidly hunkering down. They are the manifestation of passion and positive energy, exhibiting a go-getting, lively spirit that all customers love. They can put a smile on your face and a skip in your step—even in moments of doubt.

The Flavors of Joy

Joyful servers come in three flavors—closers, singers, and fireflies. *Closers* are the version of joy-giver that gets things done for customers. Too often customers witness service people who focus only on doing their task without regard to the customer's objective. As long as they can "check the box" that their part of the service chain was done, they seem indifferent to the overall result. Joyful service people, on the other hand, care about outcomes, not about checklists. Activity is a means to an end, not an end in itself. Procedures are guidelines for accomplishment, not the goal itself.

Erik Becerra, team leader for AMEX World Service in Mexico City, had a card member request a supplementary card for his wife, who was about to travel from Mexico to the United States. However, the card was not going to reach her in time for her early morning flight. Erik spent hours trying to arrange a same-day delivery, even consulting with contacts at connecting and destination airports to see if they could serve as pick-up points. Nothing was working out. So, Erik drove three hours to the card member's home to personally deliver the card at 2:30 a.m. the morning of the flight. Not surprisingly, the president of American Express Mexico received a letter from a very happy customer.

Another flavor of joyful servers is the singer. *Singers* make customers feel confident about the parts of their service encounter they sometimes do not understand. The mechanic under the hood might speak internal combustion techno babble, but when delivered with upbeat confidence it helps us trust that our transmission was treated with TLC. Insurance has "fine-print" parts for many customers; joyful service helps customers trust service people to be their advocates, not bureaucracy wardens.

Tom Berger has been Chip's family financial consultant for more than fifteen years. His greatest asset is not just his 24/7 attention to the Bells' financial affairs nor his willingness to go the extra mile on every financial service he provides. All these are accurate features of one of Merrill Lynch's finest. Tom's special gift is his zeal to be a passionate mentor. And, he prepares as diligently as he serves. Great service providers bubble over with pride when witnessing the byproducts of their instructive service. When the partnership-steered portfolio performs well, Tom is as thrilled as the Bells. He steps back in innocent awe that the investment strategy worked—again. The whole joy of serving seems to propel him to make the next investment one-up the last one.

Our favorite flavor of joyful server is the firefly. *Fireflies* go after spirit leeches. One of the hazards of fishing swampy rivers is the risk of attracting a leech. A ritual among river anglers is to always check for the bloodsuckers after emerging from the water. And, the typical way to remove the slimy hitchhiker is with a lighted match or lighter. Leeches suck the blood from their target; spirit leeches suck the energy and passion from theirs. Some spirit leeches are dark creatures—removing optimism, hope, and confidence. Mention an opportunity and they can tell you why it's a mistake. Others are almost invisible—specializing in putting wet blankets on joy. Spirit leeches are removed the same way real leeches are—with fire. Not a real match, of course, but with the warmth and energy of spirit. And, that is where the firefly version of the joyful server comes in handy.

Go to

Getting "you" grounded and ready to partner with customers includes working collaboratively with your colleagues. Tool #3 provides insights for making colleague relationships work better, so together you can better serve the customer.

You do not inherit spirit, acquire spirit, or borrow spirit. You choose spirit much as you choose to introduce yourself to a stranger. Those who opt for an upbeat, positive spirit are happier, healthier, and more productive. And, they refuse to let spirit leeches attach to them. Fireflies are service providers who choose the light over the fog. Most servers don't opt for the dark, but they tolerate a fog—that endless chain of boring, eventless moments. Fireflies demonstrate the courage to glow by showing zero tolerance for fog or compliance with the party poopers and spoilsports. Fireflies know that if they show spirit leeches their joyful side they get to watch them disappear!

Customer tranquility requires service providers who are experts in creating harmony. Calm comes to customers when they feel valued by a server who is focused on them and their needs. They feel special when they are served by one who is generous. And, they feel confident when their server seeks to create a joyful experience.

/\/\/\/

A very gloomy *Wall Street Journal* on a very long flight left Chip with a very bad headache. Chip never gets headaches! As soon as he exited the jetway at the San Francisco Airport, he headed for the nearest newsstand for some pain relief. The vendor was about to close but Chip talked him into selling him his last package of headache pills.

Chip opened the plastic package and removed the two tablets in foil for some quick relief. Tucked behind the foil in the shrink wrapped package was a collapsible paper cup just big enough for two large swallows of water.

Chip laughed out loud to see such genius! "Why can't everyone serving customers be like this two-swallow gift?" he thought. It was a focused, generous and joyful surprise. He could almost feel his headache start to dissipate, and he hadn't even taken the pain relievers.

Why not give customers a "two-swallow paper cup"? That cup might take the form of much longer patience when a customer frets over minutiae. It might be a sincere, unexpected smile. It might be a random act of kindness targeted at a familiar service challenge—a long wait time, a crowded checkout line, or laborious required paperwork. David Harris was our "two-swallow paper cup." And, his focus, generosity and joyful manner turned our anxiety into admiration.

CHAPTER 8

Connection
How to Help Customers Feel Like Partners

> To give real service you must add something which
> cannot be bought or measured with money, and that
> is sincerity and integrity.
>
> Donald A. Adams

How many times have you looked at a product or service and said to yourself "I wish I'd thought of that"? Today's winning organizations—the ones with the endearing and enduring products and services—design them "with" customers rather than "for" customers. The "for" group creates a product or service and then conducts market research, including focus groups to get customers' reactions for refinement. "I prefer the blue one over the green one" or "I would like it better if it was sweeter or faster, or whatever." The customer is viewed as judge and jury, not as partner.

The "with" group, on the other hand, views and treats customers as true partners in the product or service life cycle. Their work starts with customers: they learn about their customers' hopes, habits, fears, and aspirations and then go to work designing. They spend time trying to get into the customer's mind—thinking deeply about the life of the product or service through their customers' lives. They include customers at early drawing-board stages, get reactions to possible product or service variations, and keep customers posted on progress from idea to implementation. They ask customers for advice on all the tough decisions. And when the product or service is finally launched, it feels to the target market like "our product." Think beta groups on steroids!

Customer connection starts with a partnership philosophy, a partnership approach, and, more important, a partnership practice. Whether you are a frontline employee serving a colleague down the hall, a department head supervising call center reps, the owner of a mom and pop enterprise, or the CEO of a large company, embedding partnering into the DNA of your work dramatically alters how you serve. Customers are influenced by a partnering outreach; their concern changes to calm, their fickleness to loyalty. Let's examine a unique and unlikely example.

How could you improve on a product as simple and pedestrian as a baby bottle? Playtex, Evenflo, Similac, Dr. Brown's, and ThinkBaby have all tweaked the hundred-year-old design with better nipples, easier handles, and ways to minimize uncomfortable air intake. But, inventor-entrepreneur Jason Tebeau took the baby bottle in a completely different direction. He created a hands-free bottle that left baby independent during feeding time.

It all started when Tebeau's mom asked him, "How do you feed a baby while in a car seat or stroller?" His inventive brain went to work thinking through the mind of the user. Assembling a group of 40 to 50 babies with parent in tow, Tebeau observed babies interacting with bottles in various stages of the design process as he solved assorted product challenges—how to work with the physics of liquid moving up a tube, how to capitalize on babies' tendencies to put everything in their mouths and treat every object as a toy, how to design an accordion-flex tube that babies could not remove, how to use a valve to retain liquid in the pacifier-style nipple so babies would not lose interest if they stopped sucking and the liquid sank back into the bottle.

The end result was the wildly popular Pacifeeder, one of several products from Tebeau's company Savi Baby. Sold at such retail outlets as Target and Amazon.com, the bottle has been so popular that many older babies prefer it over the traditional "lie in mommy's lap" variety. The customers—babies and their parents—were intimately involved throughout. Tebeau even used parents to help determine the appropriate price for his creative product, knowing retailers might see it as "just another baby bottle."

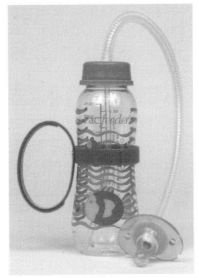

Photo courtesy of Savi Baby

As customers, we all get told a lot that we are important and valued. Yet, the proof of our worth too often is little more than PR noise and advertising taglines. Customers know actions speak louder than words; the tangible evidence of worth lies in what an organization does, not in what it says. Customers as partners mean finding ways to treat customers so they know they are valued, not just testifying that they are. And, the epitome of partnership is inclusion.

So, what is the main take-away from a "with" approach versus a "for" approach? Whether tangible product or intangible service, embedding the customer into the DNA rebalances the service covenant with connection. But as central as inclusion is to partnering, the success of collaboration requires other ingredients to make it work and ensure it lasts.

What Makes Partnering Work

We have moved our respective families many times. Chip's most recent cross-country move was in the last five years. One of the first initiatives in the new locale was to assemble "the team." His family researched to find an array of professionals—a carpenter, dentist, painter, doctors, plumber, electrician, roofer, and landscaper. They also selected a favorite grocery, dry cleaner, hairdresser, hardware store, and other product/service providers.

WHAT PARTNERSHIP IS NOT!

- Partnership is not a passenger in luggage claim seeking their own baggage. It is about the alliance.
- Partnership is not a raging bull. It is having a long fuse.
- Partnership is not being a news anchor. It is about keeping secrets.
- Partnership is not an accountant balancing the books. It is about forgiveness and floating reciprocity.
- Partnership is not for quitters. Partners are tenacious and stay on purpose.

Zachery Kail
Adapted from a wedding sermon

Over the first few months, some of Chip's family's providers are fired and replaced as they refine the team, all with great customer service skills, easy access, responsive attitudes, and a commitment to a partnership relationship. Standards are high. And, the pace with which the family replaces a failed relationship is rapid. However, the rewards for being on the team are worthwhile—Chip is a generous tipper (why wouldn't you tip your plumber?) and the family's loyalty to the team is unfailing. Chip does not shop the competition each time he needs a sink replaced or a tooth filled. He is their advocate to others seeking a resource.

Take a quick look at the most recent "Best Companies for Customer Service" lists.[1] The same cast of characters makes those lists year in, year out. What do Publix, Wegmans, Ace Hardware, Nordstrom, and Starbucks have in common? They are brick-and-mortar companies that deliver service largely face to face. What do L.L. Bean, Amex, Chas. Schwab, and USAA have in common? They deliver service largely ear to ear. And, what do Zappos, Dell, and Amazon have in common? You know where this is going. They deliver services largely on the Internet.

Now, what do they all have in common? Regardless of their primary channel of service delivery, they have built a powerful bond with customers by bringing partnership principles to the service experience. They all have unmistakable features that bring back into their service covenant with customers those elements that have been stripped out or convoluted by many service providers. Their bottom-line performance is part of the payoff. But, the biggest benefit is the huge collection of loyal fans who buy more, buy more often, forgive more, and advocate more.

The Truth, the Whole Truth, and . . .

The Delta regional jet was packed. As the flight backed away from the gate, the flight attendant began her ritualistic safety spiel about seatbelts, sudden turbulence, and smoking. She ended by saying, "The flying time to Grand Rapids will be two hours . . . no, it will be an hour-and-a-half . . . no, actually, I don't know." The cabin erupted with laughter and applause.

What jolted the half-asleep plane-full into cheering? Unscripted, raw truth-telling. We all loved her total candor and confident authenticity!

We all grow up hearing "Honesty is the best policy." As adults we hear half-truths portrayed as honesty. Politicians keep secret the number of paramilitary civilians fighting in a trouble spot to disguise the true size of the military engagement—a number they know the public would not tolerate. The super-low price loudly advertised comes with fine print describing a rebate paid only after submitting a pound of paper work. And, when we hear the radio ad end with a fast-talking guy rattling off all the exceptions and disclaimers, we know we are not hearing raw honesty.

Customers love honesty, especially when circumstances might have others shading the truth or withholding the facts. JetBlue went from joke material to exemplar status after the super-long tarmac delay in Denver because the company CEO hid nothing. Toyota got hammered because they seemed to do the opposite when a malfunctioning accelerator was sticking and causing wrecks. Both had sterling reputations before their visits to PR hell.

Car dealers are rarely on the "most honest industry" list. Yet, Manheim, the largest wholesale auto auction company in North America, has a phenomenally positive reputation because integrity is more than a corporate value engraved on the wall (as Enron had at their corporate headquarters). Integrity is a way of life engraved in the hearts and habits of employees. Since we have consulted with Manheim for several years, we have repeatedly witnessed that "the right thing to do" always trumped "the most profitable" or "least difficult" or "most convenient."

Honesty shortens the distance between people. It frees customers from anxiety and caution. It triggers a connection with the humanity in each of us. In that space we are quicker to forgive, more tolerant of error, and much more accepting of "Actually, I don't know." Honesty is not a "best policy." Honesty is a "best practice."

Be As Fair As Your Mother Taught You to Be

"When *Business Week* picks Amazon.com as the #1 best service company—an online fulfillment company—it is proof good old-fashioned service is dead." The comment sounded like a "kids are going to the dogs" statement someone's grandfather might make. But, it was coming from a non–computer savvy physician in one of our client focus groups.

Suddenly others in the room jumped into the discussion with jubilant praise for Amazon.com. "Their website is so easy," "I always get what I order," "Their prices are the best," and "Returns are a breeze." Their comments reflected excellence at the basics—the core expectations, all the shoulda's and oughta's. But then someone told the story of a customer ordering a used book through Amazon.com, not getting the book expected, with zero success contacting the used-book company. Amazon not only refunded the customer's money before the flawed book was returned but also took on the rogue used-book dealer on behalf of the customer. "Maybe I was wrong," said the nay-saying doctor quietly. "I didn't know there was fair play still playing in the business world these days."

All service begins with an expectation of fairness. Read that sentence again—it is vital to understanding customer partnerships. Customers enter the service experience with preconceived ideas about what should happen. When the experience approximates the expectation, the customer is in emotional balance. In the past, customers assumed the service world would treat them fairly.

Today's customers are twice burned. The problem is not that they completely lack trust that things will turn out well, or at least okay. It is that their experience has warned them that a more cautious, guilty-until-proven-innocent stance is wiser. As the old adage goes, "Fool me once, shame on you. Fool me twice, shame on me."

Fairness is what we teach little leaguers, Boy Scouts and Girl Scouts, the neighborhood soccer team. "It's not whether you win or lose," we tell them, "it is how you play the game." Little tikes just learning to throw or kick the ball get an end-of-the-season trophy just for being on the team. Our marriage vows are filled with fairness words—"in good times and bad times; in sickness and in health." Fairness is doing the right thing for both parties. It is a governor on greed and the control on conceit. It keeps us engulfed in consideration when all around us entices us to be selfish.

Build Shock Absorbers into the Relationship

Great partnerships are highly elastic and adaptable. Elastic customer relationships have built-in shock absorbers. They expand and unfold in their acceptance; little bumps in the road of service interactions are absorbed without throwing servers off their game. A partnering spirit is about affirming relationships more through ebb and flow than give and take. It encourages elbow room rather than close inspection; it seeks ways to open rather than a means to close. Instead of nitpicking details, great partners work to roll with anticipated imperfections, or unexpected waves of discontent.

"Thank you for being my customers," the shop owner said to a group of prospects who seemed to be loitering in his small store at the mall. What was unique about his statement was that it was directed at three teenagers, each with a very loud disposition, extremely baggy pants, and earphones hooked up to an iPod. Out of earshot of the owner, one young man remarked to his buddies, "Man, we *gotta* buy something!" As they left the checkout counter, the store owner shot point blank one last blast of benevolence: "Please visit me again."

Service with soul is service that is elastic enough to give new depth, meaning, and substance to the encounter. It reflects a commitment to respect and generosity. It is an assertion, not a response; an attitude, not a tactic. We get a glimpse of the tone when we witness a "random act of kindness." Except elasticity is not random, it is continual. As with those teenagers at the mall, it causes customers to act their best. It can tame hostility, enrich the ordinary, and deliver real value in the service experience.

Since most customers come into the encounter expecting disappointment, how can we surprise them in a fashion that says "This is different"? What is the anatomy of service value? It is three things: being really good, eliminating the hassles, and adding a surprise.

Fly Your Customer's Flag

The tall, rugged Russian wholesale auto buyer could barely speak English. But, his passion for his export business was glaring to anyone within a block. We were consulting with a large auto auction company to help them create a new service uniquely crafted for wholesale buyers who purchased vehicles at U.S. auctions specifically to ship them overseas to be sold by auto retailers. Our interviews were conducted at particular auto auctions that had a large customer base of exporters.

"Why do you like this particular auction?" we asked the Russian buyer. "They fly my flag!" he proudly announced. Later we visited the auction lanes where buyers and sellers gathered around several seemingly never-ending rows of cars with an auctioneer at each lane refereeing the auto marketplace. Along the upper wall of the giant warehouse flew a United Nations-like row of national flags, one for each country represented by the customers present at the auction.

"Flying your customer's flag" is more than a symbol of personalization; it is a sign of deep and obvious respect. Respect can come in the form of honesty and fairness. It can be a compassionate deference to a customer's unique circumstance and special interests. But, its liveliest form is found in the exceptions that are grounded in customer understanding and fueled by generosity. "We don't normally, but in your case," "I went ahead and took care of that," or "I comped the charge since I knew. . . ." are all the sounds of customer-centric exceptions.

Exceptions tell customers you are there for *them*, not just for you. Customers want you to be successful and profitable; they do not want you to be miserly or greedy. Rigid commerce fails to accommodate the humanness of serving. Exceptions telegraph to customers there is a partnership governing the rules of engagement, not a programmed computer or frontline employee.

Give More Than Customers Expect

Great partners give without condition; giving is a selfless act. For the service provider, it is service emanating from the inner joy of serving, not a calculated decision. It requires a focus, not on short-term financial benefit but on long-term relationship value. While transaction costs are not irrelevant, they can become destructively dominant. Of course, there are some fickle customers on the prowl for a cheap "one-night stand" they can brag about as a financial conquest. But effective partners know that such customers are a tiny minority and it's folly to distrust the balance of clients because of the few who seek to "game" the system. They understand that by seeking win-win solutions and avoiding nickel-and-diming customers to death, their organization will be rewarded with grateful and devoted customers who return again and again, often with friends or family in tow.

Bob Miller, manager of the First Watch Restaurant in Kansas City, purchased a large supply of umbrellas for his customers. Attaching his business card to each one, he put them in a large container at the front door along with a sign that read: "If you need an umbrella, please take one. If you bring it back, we'll give you a free cup of coffee."

Freeman, a company headquartered in Dallas, Texas, provides services for exhibitions, conventions, and corporate events. Attend any large trade show around the country and odds are Freeman has supplied much of the furnishings and merchandise you see around you. Freeman developed Concierge Elite as a way to service their customers from the comforts of their booth rather than requiring them to leave the exhibit floor to visit the Freeman Service Center. The Freeman concierge visits customers on the show floor with a mobile device to assist them by looking up freight information, placing new orders, and submitting service requests for all vendors. Customers receive a text message alerting them when their requests and/or concerns are resolved, allowing them to focus on their booth and their customers.

Freeman customers liked Concierge Elite but Freeman elected to give them more. For example, customers wanted a mobile solution so they could be more interactive with Freeman. Concierge Elite now offers customers the convenience of self-service from their smart phone, mobile device, or PC. Exhibitors can sign up to receive text alerts when their freight has arrived, view current booth orders, submit service requests, and find out when empty containers are returned after the show closes. At the close of the event, customers can also request shipping labels (which Freeman hand delivers to them!) and submit their paperwork for shipping their materials back without ever spending time walking to and waiting at the Freeman Service Center.

The pursuit of generosity exemplified in Freeman helps service providers think differently about customers; connections are more personal, communications more attentive. It also causes employees to think creatively about every aspect of their role, not just those related to serving the customer. Finally, when people are a part of a culture that strives for generous service, there is a greater sense of passion conferred on customers who reciprocate with their affirmation, gratitude, and devotion.

And, Never Take the Customer for Granted

We checked into the Lake Lure Inn. Built in 1927, the antique North Carolina hotel served as command central for the making of the movie *Dirty Dancing*. You now can stay in the Patrick Swayze Suite or the Jennifer Grey Suite. Furnished with exquisite period furniture and meticulous attention to detail, the surroundings make guests feel elevated, enchanted, and enriched.

We had dinner in their Veranda Restaurant overlooking the lake, only a stone's throw away from our table. The staff was all locals from the small mountain town. They reached way beyond their plain heritage in a noticeable effort to create a sense of elegance and worth. After seating us at our reserved table, the maitre d' presented the menus and wine list, and then graciously said, "Hope ya'll enjoy"—not a phrase you'd hear at a five-star restaurant in Boston or San Francisco. There was an earnest effort to take the experience much, much higher than you would get at Nettie's Diner down the street where the wait staff simply performs their tasks.

The difference between the Lake Lure Inn and Nettie's Diner came primarily from a deliberate attempt to not take the customer for granted. Someone decided that this classy hotel setting should come with an equally classy guest experience. Knowing they could not afford to import a Ritz-Carlton Hotel–trained wait staff, they entrusted their valuable reputation to young people recruited from the local Burgers and More. Then they trained them to not take the guest for granted but make their experience consistently and perpetually as elegant as the old hotel.

The next morning we were in too much of a hurry to wait for the hotel's Sunday brunch, featuring eggs Florentine and fresh mountain trout. So, we stopped at Nettie's for scrambled eggs, bacon, grits, and biscuits. The food was just as we expected—completely routine, plain vanilla, nothing out of the ordinary. As we looked at the Lake Lure Inn in the distance, we suddenly realized that, had we stopped at Nettie's first when we came to town, the diner might not have seemed so plain vanilla. The Lake Lure Inn had altered our service expectations and Nettie's would never be the same again—nor would any other service provider for that matter.

Do customers want every service experience to be a Lake Lure Inn moment? Maybe not, but they do want something special. Customers in 2010 research by Convergys, for example, registered their preferences for knowledgeable people, first-call resolution, and web chat capability, to name a few.[2] When the data was sliced and diced by segments—gender, age, and so forth—insights deepened regarding the way customers prefer to connect with a service provider.

Go to

This is the most important chapter in the book. It outlines the core of connecting like a partner. It is likely all the content will not be new. We hope all is renewal. In Part Three: Favorites, "Twenty Things Today's Wired and Dangerous Customers Really Want" may enrich your thinking about customers as partners.

For the two of us, the most fascinating tidbit teased out of the data implied that the path back to loyalty was to rebalance the service covenant. The most loyal customers (about 15 percent) were very different from other customers. Super-loyal advocates favored human-based interactions with live phone agents and live chat with web agents. In return for their revenue-generating loyalty and advocacy, they expected easy, rapid access to agents.[3] Even in an era of Internet-driven, fast-moving, automated service, the most loyal customers still want a service covenant that lets them co-create the experience on an equal footing with the service provider. It's not that they want to be treated as we were at Lake Lure. It's that they long for a partnership.

PROPERTY OF THE LIBRARY
YORK COUNTY COMMUNITY COLLEGE
112 COLLEGE DRIVE
WELLS, MAINE 04090
(207) 646-9282

Bad Connections

How to Turn Angry Customers into Partners

Service is a performance, much like a stage play. Put yourself in the audience of the one-act service play to follow.

Act 1, Scene 1:
The Service Desk at Acme Encore:
Used Computers, New Software & Fast Repairs

"I bought a new accounting software package and I can't get it to load," the well-dressed, gray-haired gentleman confided to the twenty-something service tech behind the service counter. John was behind him in line waiting to pick up a repaired laptop computer left the previous week.

"You probably loaded it wrong," the service tech snapped, without looking up from the paperwork he was completing. The customer moved forward, raised himself several inches taller, and peered down with obvious disdain at the young tech.

"What do you mean I loaded it wrong! Young man, I've been loading computer programs since the Macintosh in '85. I think it's the computer your company sold me two months ago." His decibel level was noticeably higher.

"Well if you bought it two months ago, the 30-day warranty is up and we can't help you anyway. You'll just have to send it to the manufacturer for repair." The service tech seemed pleased to pass the customer and his problem on down the line.

"No! That's not good enough," said the now clearly angry customer. "You sold me a defective product and now you are making me do all the work. I want to talk to your boss."

"You can talk all you want to, mister, but it won't change our policies. Now, please let me deal with the next customer." Being the next customer in line, John was really thrilled by the prospect of being this smug little critter's next victim!

Act 1, Scene 2:
Acme Encore—The Boss's Office

"Mr. Careless will see you now," the receptionist said as she escorted the angry customer into the boss's office.

"How can I help you, sir?" said Mr. Careless as he greeted the upset customer.

"You can start by firing that sorry *@# tech on your service desk. He was rude, disrespectful, and completely uninterested in helping me, or, for that matter, caring about your reputation!"

You could almost hear the boss thinking, "We have a very bad connection!"

Curtain closes.

Ever wonder why electricians refer to an ineffective electrical connection as a "bad" connection, like it was misbehaving and in need of punishment? It is how many service providers view angry customers—not as someone who has experienced a failed service connection, but as the perpetrator of a "bad" connection. As long as the customer with a beef is viewed as "bad" rather than "injured," the more efforts to right the customer connection will simply short-circuit.

Bad connections happen! Fortunately, today's customers, as restless, short-tempered, and impatient as they may be, do not expect service providers to be perfect. They know service is powered through human relationships and "To err is human." They do expect organizations always to demonstrate they care in the face of any customer disappointment. In the words of renowned author and Texas A&M professor Len Berry, "The acid test of service quality is how you solve customers' problems."[1]

Fixing Problems vs. Healing Relationships

The field of service recovery has had a rather sordid history. Recall some of the super-botched recovery examples—Ford Explorer, the Exxon *Valdez*, the BP Gulf oil spill—and you discover that someone at the helm likely determined that service recovery was all about damage control, not about customer healing. Without fixing the disappointed customer, all manner of physical repair of the customer's issue will be for naught.

Everyone who has frequented a fast food restaurant has had the experience of the drive-in or counter clerk occasionally getting the order wrong. Say, you ordered a large fries but you received a small fries instead. As customers, we know there will be an occasional error, especially in a setting where speed is a factor. We don't go to a quick service establishment for slow service. The memorable part is how they handle the hiccup. If the server makes no eye contact, registers no remorse, and shows zero empathy, even if the incorrect order is corrected, as customers, we end up angrier than we were with the initial mistake.

Fixing the customer's problem is crucial. That is what customers assume will happen. It is emotional healing that trumps problem repair. As the oft-quoted line goes: "Customers don't care how much you know until they know how much you care." It is the relationship side, not the engineering side, of service recovery that keeps service providers off the "don't go there" list.

If customer healing is emotional, it is beneficial to examine what is happening in the customers' minds behind their feelings of disdain, disappointment, or anger. Let's take a tour inside that mind, looking at what's going on from the customer end of a bad connection.

All service experiences begin with an expectation of fairness. When things go sour, for whatever reason, customers also have preconceived ideas about what should happen to set things right. Customers of a utility have different standards for recovery during a storm than when the same outage occurs because the power company goofed.

When their recovery experience approximates their recovery expectation, the customer is in emotional balance. As we earlier noted, most—though certainly not all—customers assume the world will treat them fairly. This is not a mark of naiveté, simply recognition that, on balance, most customers have more life experiences that fall on the "fair" than on the "not fair" side of the ledger.

So when a service provider acts in a manner the customer deems unfair, customers feel betrayed—an implied promise was not honored and the service covenant has thus been violated. What is critical to great recovery is an understanding that customers' views of the world are always accurate and reasonable from their point of view, not necessarily from the viewpoint of the service provider. As the country adage goes, "It is easier to turn a mule if you first get the mule moving." Starting where the customer is, getting in their shoes, is tantamount to guiding them to a happy ending. In the customer's eyes, you are not qualified to change their view until you first demonstrate you completely understand their view.

Customers *do* make mistakes, and they know they make mistakes. But whether they caused the error themselves, it was an act of nature, or the organization was the cause, they assume their view of what should happen after a service hiccup is the only right, or reasonable, course of action. When that view is directly challenged or questioned in any way, customers don't just assume their challenger is wrong; they see it as an attempt to control, prevail, coerce, or engage in all manner of unrighteous action.

The Psycho-Logic of Customer Healing

Understanding the customer's emotional state when events veer far off their anticipated course, when an expected right turn suddenly becomes a left, is an essential first step in balancing the "status quo," as

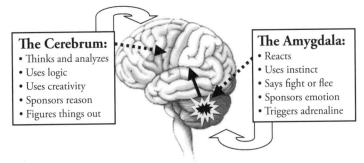

The Cerebrum:
- Thinks and analyzes
- Uses logic
- Uses creativity
- Sponsors reason
- Figures things out

The Amygdala:
- Reacts
- Uses instinct
- Says fight or flee
- Sponsors emotion
- Triggers adrenaline

Figure 3. The Human Brain's Cerebrum and Amygdala

Jon Voight's *National Treasure* character would say. It is at this point where who is right or who is wrong begins to take a backseat. It is also the point when the customer's unique perspective on the problem at hand must be heard, understood, and respected.

Now, let's take a deep dive into the psycho-logic of service recovery. We begin with a review of what you probably learned in ninth-grade general science or tenth-grade biology about the workings of the brain. The brain is divided into many parts. We will focus on two key parts—the cerebrum and the amygdala (see Figure 3). The cerebrum is that big grey wrinkly part that we typically call the brain. It is divided into two halves (or hemispheres)—the right side is the intuitive, creative side; the left is the logical, rational side.

What does the cerebrum do? In its entirety it is the seat of logic, creativity, analysis, insight, learning, and problem-solving. We humans have the largest cerebrum in relation to body weight of any species. In fact, the label *Homo sapiens* comes from the Latin meaning "wise or knowing man."

And, the amygdala? From an evolutionary perspective, it is one of the oldest parts of the brain and controls instinct and a person's physical reaction to danger. Sometimes referred to as the reptilian brain (or, with a hat tip to Seth Godin, the lizard brain), it controls the fight-or-flight response and triggers the secretion of adrenaline—the hormone that gets dumped into the bloodstream to make us faster, stronger, and tougher when threatened. Adrenaline is not stored in the brain, but it is the amygdala that flips the switch causing its release. It is what makes your hair stand on end and enables all your senses to be much sharper and keener in a crisis.

When you experience anything in life, imagine the message taking two routes. The slower route goes to the cerebrum; the faster route goes to the amygdala (refer to Figure 3). The amygdala is connected to the cerebrum and acts much like an early-warning clearinghouse for any signs of threat. If the amygdala senses danger, it quickly sends a message to the cerebrum requesting it to ignore the forthcoming message (the slower-moving information). With that warning, the cerebrum mostly shuts down—sometimes as much as two-thirds of it—in order to allow the amygdala to deal with the threat situation in a reactive or instinctive way. In other words, evolution has enabled the brain to let instinct rule over logic in times of threat or danger.

Imagine a cave man out on a leisurely stroll when he suddenly encounters a mean, angry saber-tooth tiger. If the cave man thought to himself, "Let me figure this out. Seems to me I recall my father telling me if I saw one of these animals I needed to move to the left, no wait, I believe it was move to the right," what do you think would happen? He'd be lunch to the saber-tooth tiger. So, the brain learned that in saber-tooth tiger situations, we will live longer if the situation is dealt with instinctively and reactively, rather than logically and rationally.

The brain works today much like it did then. That is why, if your boss comes in and screams, "What the hell is this?" it is like a saber-tooth tiger to your brain and you find yourself getting suddenly very stupid. Actually, today it is not the threat of physical harm that triggers the amygdala's taking over for the cerebrum; it is the threat of emotional harm, which can range in severity from mild disappointment to downright fury. The more the sense of harm moves to the fury end, the more "victim" the customer feels.

The path to getting a good connection is to remember the customer is not acting rational, but acting threatened. There is an old truism in psychology that states: anger is not a primary behavior, it is a secondary behavior. The primary behavior is fear. What we see on the outside might be anger; what is going on in the mind of the angry customer is fear. So, when your customer is very angry, ask yourself: "What is he or she afraid of?" Bottom line, it is the fear of being a victim.

What does being a victim really mean to a customer? It could mean many things: "I will look stupid," "I will lose control," "You will win and I will lose," "I will lose now but I'll lose even more next time." You get the idea.

The point is, when people go into this state, they are not operating out of their normal thinking brain. They are operating out of the world of fight-or-flight—they want to fight or flee. They may appear to be acting practically insane. Actually, at some level, their irrational response is a type of temporary insanity. The logic of customer healing is to invite the person out of their "insane" state to a more rational state where effective and joint problem solving can occur. Think of the right-balancing goal as an invitation to partner.

Partners Soothe, They Don't Defend

Imagine you are the parent of a small child who wakes up in the middle of the night frightened by a bad dream. In tears, the child comes into your bedroom. What would you do and say? The answer is easy—you would model bravery and confidence; you would carefully listen without judgment; and, you would offer great empathy as you seek to calm and encourage. The principles used for a small child with a bad dream are the same for customers with a bone to pick.

Angry customers feel victimized in some way. The source of the fury may vary. We all have our hot-button triggers hardwired to early experiences and learnings, albeit sometimes causing irrational beliefs. Regardless of what's driving the customer's sense of victimization, the response should demonstrate the complete absence or even hint of threat. The attitude reflected by the service provider should always be one that reflects the "3 Cs"—calm, confident, and competent. A calm attitude will help to reflect humility and the attitude you want from the customer. A confident attitude will soothe because in the tense early stages of recovery you want the customer to know you can handle their situation. A competent attitude is essential because you must not just fix the customer, you must actually be able to fix the problem.

Another essential in partner-like soothing is **humility,** our label for sincere compassion, authentic concern, and total vulnerability. Humility is crucial in the service provider's response to an angry customer because it communicates "I am not your enemy." It announces a kind of no-fight zone in order to calm the raging customer out of the "ready to fight" amygdala-driven mode. It begins with creating a connection that demonstrates sincere interest and obvious concern. Use open posture and eye contact. Listen to the customer and, equally important, look as if you are listening. Apologize with feeling. Avoid using *we* in apologizing to customers, as in "We're sorry." Apology should always be delivered in first-person singular: "I'm sorry." "I'm sorry" doesn't suggest you caused the problem or that you're automatically the culprit. "I'm sorry" does mean, however, "I care." It says you are not just passing along the sentiments of some anonymous or impersonal *we* looming in the background.

The tone chosen is equally important. Again, model the attitude you would like the customer to assume. As Abraham Lincoln said, "A person convinced against their will is of the same opinion still." Assume innocence, even if you have prior history about this angry customer. Lower your voice. Let the customer witness genuine concern. If you are in a face-to-face recovery situation, look the customer in the eye. Be forthright and direct. There's no need for a "tail between your legs" style. Things went wrong; the customer was disappointed. Acknowledge it honestly and frankly, and be ready to learn from it and move on.

Partners Understand, They Don't Justify

It is important to remember that, before you can engage the customer in problem-solving, you must get them out of the part of the brain they are currently in (the amygdala) and into the part of their brain where problem-solving occurs (the cerebrum). The amygdala is telling them to get ready for a fight. The actions of the service provider need to signal that the customer's defensive stance is not necessary. Humility begins to set the stage, but it is the search for understanding that causes the customer to shift from the fight-or-flight posture to problem-solving mode.

Empathy is an expression of kinship and a powerful partnering practice. It says to the customer that you are like the customer—not above or below. It means using words that communicate complete identification with the customer; that you fully appreciate the impact the service failure has had on them. It is like saying "I get it! I know just how much this hurts. I am in tune with where you are, and I would feel just like you do if this had happened to me."

It is important to show confidence while demonstrating empathy. In other words, it is inappropriate for service people to wallow in bad feelings or demonstrate a "we goofed up big-time" sentiment. Remember, empathy is not synonymous with sympathy. Customers don't want someone to cry with (sympathy or shared weakness); they want an understanding shoulder to cry on (empathy or the gift of strength).

Empathy communicates understanding and identification. It means listening to learn, not listening to make a point or to correct. Whether you as a service provider agree or disagree with the customer's view isn't the point. The goal is to give evidence that you understand. It includes agreeing with their feelings (not necessarily their position). Deal with feelings, before you deal with facts.

THE SERVICE DOCTOR SAYS

H Humility. Let customers hear your sincere concern. "I am so sorry . . ."

E Empathy. Let customers hear words that communicate "I can appreciate why you are upset."

A Alliance. Let customers witness your sense of urgency. Offer a symbolic gesture of sorrow if appropriate.

L Loyalty. Let customers know you care by following up after a problem

Understanding customers in times of trial and tribulation includes getting insight into their expectations. If a solution or repair to the service covenant is in the offing, knowing the customer's expectation for resolution is vital. A customer's expectations can be as unique as the body shape and inner functioning a patient presents to a doctor. But just as in medicine, there are fundamental similarities that can guide our efforts. The basic likeness of two different human's kidneys enables physicians to perform kidney surgery using a reliable set of norms, protocols, and prognoses. There is an apt parallel in service recovery expectations. We all want personalized treatment, but our individual visions of what that entails can share a lot of similarities. Think of your role as that of a service doctor.

Partners Include, They Don't Impose

Assuming you have drawn the person out of the victim state, the customer is now more in a partnership position for joint problem solving. However, the reason we stay focused on a mutual discovery process is because the customer's trust in you is still very tenuous and cautious. Therefore, to offer a solution can be less effective than finding a solution together. **Alliance** is the word we use for the type of partnership-driven collective problem-solving required.

Alliances are formed through give and take. They are achieved through joint discovery. Language like "What would you suggest?" or "What would you like to happen next?" is more inclusive and less threatening than "off-the-shelf"–sounding solutions. Keep in mind this is about problem solving with a partner.

Alliance includes words and actions that tell customers they're dealing with someone who has the moves and the moxie to fix their problem. They want can-do competence, attentive urgency, and a take-charge, "I'll turn this around" attitude. Service failure first and foremost robs customers of the confidence they have in an organization, yet that confidence is quickly restored if customers observe you moving nimbly and confidently to address their problem.

If the infraction is major, forging an alliance may mean more than clearing up the "old debt." It may be helpful to offer some type of atonement. Atonement involves providing some token or symbolic gesture that tangibly telegraphs your sincere regret that the disappointment occurred. Atonement does not mean "buying" the problem. It can be as simple as a small courtesy, a personal extra, or a value-added favor. Act responsible for their recovery and never duck the issue or pass the buck for someone else to handle.

Partners Care, They Don't Control Damage

Assuming a solution is found and agreed upon, it is vital the customer witness something happening that communicates irrefutable proof that you can be relied on again. Healing service recovery includes **loyalty**, the after-the-fact experiences of the customer that communicate: "We are loyal to you. We will not abandon you now that we've solved your problem; this is not a one-time fix-and-forget."

Service research shows that following-up with customers who've experienced problems is one of the most powerful steps you can take to cement a continuing relationship.[2] Pick up the phone and call the customer to find out if everything is back to normal, or if there have been any continuing problems. Send the customer an email. For example, after a two-hour weather-related delay, Delta Airlines sent a short e-survey with questions specifically targeted at learning from the disappointing situation. Customers could choose which airport personnel to whom they directed their feedback (the departure city or the arrival city).

When the customer returns for future service, ask about the last problem. If customers know you remember and are still concerned, they'll come to realize their bad experience was an exception. And, remember to always keep your promises. Service recovery starts with a broken promise (at least in the eyes of the customer). Don't make a promise as a way to recover and then create doubled anger by disappointing the customer again.

/\\\/\\/

Correcting a bad connection begins and ends with remembering you are a memory-maker. Memory making is about how we turn customer disappointment into customer delight; it is about how we transform an "oops" into an opportunity, turning a bad connection into a good one. Most of all, it is the recognition that the service covenant has been broken and must be repaired, not simply patched up.

A good electrician will tell you that bonding a bad connection is only effective when the repair is made stronger than the original. The same is true for service recovery. Research tells us that customers who have a problem and have that problem spectacularly solved will be more loyal than customers who have never even had a problem.[3]

Go to

To err is human! And, you cannot please everyone all the time. Tool #1 provides ways to deal with those uniquely challenging customers. Tool #10 can help you deal with that (we hope) very rare situation in which you have to part ways with a customer.

Think of it like this: before customers experience disappointment they operate purely on faith that all will go well. After they have experienced service breakdown followed by great recovery, they operate on proof—solid evidence that they have seen you at your worst and witnessed how effectively you right a wrong. This does not mean we want to create a problem just so we can fix it real good! It does mean that dealing like a great partner with customers at their darkest moment can be the most powerful part of memory-making.

CHAPTER 10

Wireless Connections
How to Partner with Customers via the Internet

In cyberspace, the First Amendment is a local
ordinance.

John Perry Barlow

Wireless is defined as the transfer of information without the use of
electrical conductors. In many ways this definition captures the blessing and the bother of Internet connections. The mobility, speed, and
ease of the Internet as a tool for "interlogue" are clearly worthwhile
assets. However, robbed of the capacity to read non-verbal information, there is great potential for misinformation and misinterpretation.
Without accurate dialogue, understanding can suffer.

One study at UCLA indicated that up to 93 percent of communication effectiveness is determined by non-verbal cues.[1] Another study
found that the impact of a performance was determined 7 percent by
the words used, 38 percent by voice quality, and 55 percent by the
non-verbal communication.[2] Stripping the lion's share of the effectiveness features from communications with customers puts enormous
burden on those factors that are left.

We elected to devote a chapter exclusively to the Internet customer because it is rapidly becoming the communication conduit of

choice. The key to turning this "dialogue in the dark" into a boon for renewing the service covenant requires the application of the partnership principles to the discourse.

The Internet is a lot like a rattlesnake. Rattlesnakes are not aggressive snakes until threatened. Then they provide a warning to their opponent in the form of an unmistakable rattle. But if the rattle is ignored they strike quickly and with a bite laced with venom that has a lasting impact on the "strikee." Successful organizations serving the wired-and-dangerous customer must be great "listeners for the rattle," intently monitoring all channels simultaneously. "Wired and dangerous" also suggests that once a rattle is heard from customers, the service provider must be prepared to react quickly, succinctly, and effectively.

Let's return with more detail to an example used earlier: the United Airlines baggage claim incident in the spring of 2008 with musician Dave Carroll. As we unfold the illustration, keep the rattlesnake metaphor in mind.

Dave was flying on tour with his band, the Sons of Maxwell, from Halifax to Omaha with a stopover in Chicago. When he was deplaning in Chicago to catch his connection to Omaha, he overheard a passenger exclaim, "My god, they're throwing guitars out there." The ground baggage crew first threw the bass guitar, then the case containing Dave's $3500 Taylor 710ce guitar. When he appealed to a flight attendant on board, she referred him to the terminal agents. Three different agents responded with indifference to Dave's concern, telling him he would have to take it up with baggage claim in Omaha.

When he finally arrived in Omaha at 2 a.m. (two hours late), there were obviously no baggage-claim employees available. From this point, Dave's saga of trying to get some restitution lasted almost a year, involving countless phone calls, forms, and emails. He was bounced from city to city and even airline to airline (Air Canada is the United Airlines alliance partner in Halifax). In frustration he turned his songwriting skills into a YouTube video performance called "United Breaks Guitars"[3] and posted it in July 2009. Since we are focusing on the Internet customer in this chapter, we will pick up on Dave's story at the point his video complaint went viral. In complete fairness, we are examining this saga through the customer's eyes without benefit of "the other side of the story" from United Airlines.

Be Flexible

In today's cyber world, the diversity of service is loudly amplified. Brick-and-mortar service restricts access largely to those customers geographically nearby. Rarely do customers drive many miles to patronize a particular store or service. Consequently, customers of brick-and-mortar commerce hail from similar neighborhoods with similar values and mores. With Internet service accessible to all, no matter their demography, geography, or ethnology, organizations with too many rules and restrictions and frontline employees with too little decision-making authority can box service providers into responding with what customers perceive as stubbornness.

Flexibility is not just an attitude at the opposite end of rigidity; it emanates from a keen understanding of the customer and a desire to adapt the offering to fit the customer. We were working with the call center of a major utility that had elected to eliminate a segment of 24/7 access to the call center for customers, forcing Sunday afternoon callers to wait until Monday morning. Their rationale: Only a handful of customers ever called then, so why worry. It seemed not to occur to them that they could easily and inexpensively have outsourced that service to a retired call center rep willing to cover the segment from home on Sunday afternoon. The cost of adding to the Monday morning handle time could have easily funded the part-timer.

Customer segments are different in terms of their Internet preference. Convergys 2010 research revealed that Millennials showed less preference for live phone support, while Baby Boomers showed increased preference. Their preference was driven in part by their growing frustration with automated phone systems. Gen-X customers indicated they were not using live web chat, email, or automated phone systems as much as they would like. They relied more heavily on live phone support because the channels they really preferred either did not exist or were not being supported in the right way.[4]

UNITED AIRLINES'S INITIAL DECISION ON DAVE'S GUITAR

Ms. Irwig at United denied Dave's claim for restitution to repair his guitar because he did not complain in the right place or at the right time. The culprit for the damage to his guitar was never in dispute!

The Convergys research also found a huge disconnect among Millennials between what they were using and what they really wanted. Fifty-four percent of Millennials said they have used or are likely to use texting for customer service; 47 percent have used or want to use social media for service; and 44 percent have used or want to use smart phone applications.[5]

Customers *do* expect live web chat to take longer than a live phone call, but if they knew it would take twice as long, 90 percent would opt to speak with a customer service rep.[6] There is no gain in providing live web chat if the customer spends 20 minutes chatting with an agent and then decides to pick up the phone and spend 10 minutes talking to another agent.

Dave Carroll described his "Rules R Us" experience with United to be like being served by automatons with one eye on the policy and another one on the cash register. The point is, no eyes seem to have been on the customer. "I'd also like to mention Ms. Irwig. She was mentioned in Song One," Dave said in a video on *The Consumerist* blog, "She was a great employee, and unflappable, and acting in the interest of the United policies that she represented."[7] Notice the focus of his comments—"the policies she represented!" And, when he shifted from face-to-face to online, his information was trapped in a silo forcing him to repeat his story over and over and over.

Be Inclusive

Buy a book from Amazon.com once, or rent a movie on NetFlix once, and on your next visit to their site the computer will suggest other books or movies you might like. "Customers assume that when they make a purchase, the record of that purchase will be readily available regardless of the channel it came from. All systems have to be synchronized," notes bestselling author Robert Spector.[8] Take a look at how many online companies have gone to "My" as the prefix for their personalization—MyFedEx, MyOfficeDepot, and the like.

All of us take that customerization dimension to be table stakes today. We have been taught by Internet providers to expect they will remember us from previous encounters, know our history, recognize our IP address, and populate screens quickly when we transit from online to web chat to live chat. We assume there will always be a trap door giving us easy access to a real person. Log on landsend.com and the bottom left side of the home page offers an 800 number, a chat online, or a button to click for "call me." The "all about me" customer expects to be included in ways beyond "Would you like to complete a survey at the end of this transaction?"

Service providers are answering that expectation with enormous creativity. For example, according to a blog on www.1to1media.com,

> High-tech networking giant Cisco recently tested the power of social media outlets with the launch of myPlanNet, a downloadable video game that allows players to assume the role of a CEO and solve business challenges using Cisco products. Although introduced using traditional live events, myPlanNet quickly gained widespread appeal among IT professionals who turned the simulation game into a B2B social media juggernaut spanning various channels worldwide. According to Cisco, the award-winning social media campaign for myPlanNet has been downloaded more than 35,000 times and has attracted more than 55,000 fans on its Facebook page.[9]

As Cisco and other innovative service providers know, collaboration is the core of partnership. Threadless.com invites their website community to vote on the coolest t-shirts designed by fellow amateurs. The winning entries become their product offerings, providing great exposure for budding designers and a sense of ownership by the community. Jackdaniels.com has a fan club called the Tennessee Squire Association. They asked squires in Texas to vote online for their favorite color (red, white, or blue) for the Jack Daniel's sponsored race car to be run in the annual Texas 500 race. Mountain Dew created a user-generated movement to launch a new product. The process (called Dewmocracy) involved more than 3 million customers in various phases of the design, development, and marketing of a new drink ultimately called White Out.[10] Kodak has a digital media team including a Chief Blogger, a Chief Listener, more than a dozen full-time staffers who cover the web, SEO, and social media, plus a network of part-time bloggers and Twitterers around the world who represent different departments of the company.[11]

UNITED AIRLINES SPEAKS

United spokeswoman Robin Urbanski declared, "His video is excellent and we plan to use it internally as a unique learning and training opportunity to ensure that all our customers receive better service. . . . This should have been fixed much sooner." One blogger responded with some advice for Dave: "Make sure you're paid the royalties every time they view it in their training classes."

---

eBay is another great example of an organization that views customers as partners. Every sixty days they invite twelve eBay users to journey to San Jose, California, to participate in the company's "Voice of the Customer" program. These select people visit almost every department to talk about ways to improve service. This focus group methodology goes one step further. Every month thereafter for six months these same users are reassembled to explore emerging issues. As users evolve from being interviewees to feeling like members of the organization, they get bolder in their input. They may come in as a "customer with a concern" but they leave as a "partner with a plan." The byproduct of these customer conversations has been important new offerings (like iPhone apps) and unique service enhancements for eBay.

eBay CEO John Donahoe put it this way: ". . . we were not as outside-in as we needed to be. Consumers are driving a lot of change and we've found ourselves better off if we learn how to take advantage of them. . . .The passion our sellers feel is a blessing. The minute they stop caring and screaming is the minute we should be concerned. We've tried to be much more genuine and authentic about listening to their feedback."[12]

Be Honest

The Internet world, being devoid of many of the usual signals we rely on to sense deception, demands absolute and complete honesty. It requires the pinnacle of transparency. Log on Bill Marriott's blog "Marriott on the Move" and you will learn about the new Marriott extended stay Execustay corporate apartment brand. You get a detailed up-close-and-personal tour of a typical apartment.[13] Marriott is a "people first" culture that places honesty as a centerpiece of the "home-like work atmosphere" they nurture. Walmart.com puts customer reviews right beside all the products they feature on their home page.

The truth-seeking component of effective partnership is that which values candor and openness. It is the dimension that honors authenticity and realness. The path to honesty in relationships is paved with risk taking. It involves the courage to ask for feedback as well as the commitment to value it in a way that is affirming to the sender. Honesty may sometimes leave relationships temporarily uncomfortable and bruised, but truth always leaves the partnership hearty and healthy. It exterminates guilt and deceit; it ennobles wholesomeness and trust-worthiness.

At its core, partnering is a commitment to a conversation with customers rather than unilateral action. If decision making is made without customer input it corrupts the service covenant. Partnering starts with asking for input. It continues with enlisting others in problem resolution rather than positioning yourself as the sole "answer person." Partnering is operating with the faith that wisdom lies within us all and that by tapping the collective brainpower of customers and associates, the organization is stronger, more responsive, and more adaptive to the ever-changing requirements of customers and employees.

Honesty is the byproduct of great conversations. Effective Internet servers nurture a vibrant community and foster listening posts. The more the Internet feels like a cyber watering hole, friendly to all as well as protector of all, the more it becomes a crucible of trust and an assembly of importance. It starts to resemble the old-fashioned marketplace where farmers brought produce to sell to merchants and consumers relied on the confidence derived from dependability. As on the Internet marketplace at its best, rotten apples were banned, devious bargain hunters were disdained. Someone just passing through town might get away with a shady deal, but returning vendors were required to be trustworthy.

Honesty requires making only promises that can be kept. And, once made, successful Internet servers pull out all the stops to keep them. When errors occur, they are quick to assume responsibility and demonstrate lightning speed in resolving them. What if United had gotten every person Dave encountered in his saga to write a letter of apology? What if Dave had been asked to be a spokesperson on the United website? What if they had invited Dave to be a guest speaker in the service and ramp operations training classes? What if they had put Dave's video on the United website along with the key lessons learned and steps in place to prevent future Dave-like occurrences? What if someone higher in the organization than public relations—someone on mahogany row—had commented in their annual report or corporate website?

Be Fair

One feature the Internet world lacks that face-to-face commerce typically contains is a tactile connection. Walk into a store to buy a new pair of shoes and you can feel the leather and the fit. Buy the same item online and, unless you are repurchasing an article that worked before, there is a risk that what you see will not match what you need. This makes fairness a much more crucial feature of the service covenant.

As we earlier mentioned, we consult with the largest wholesale auto auction company in the country. Buyers and sellers come together at the auto version of the "farmer's market." Major rental car companies are there to unload last year's models, auto manufacturers are there to deplete glutted inventory of a model that undersold projections, and banks are there to sell leased or repossessed vehicles. Used-car dealers are there as buyers of fresh inventory for their lots. If there is a dispute over a vehicle bought that was not as promised ("There was frame damage your inspector totally missed!"), arbitration is onsite to resolve buyer-seller disputes.

When the company elected to provide a portal that would enable buyers to watch auctions online and bid along with buyers onsite, the importance of full disclosure and fair dealings ratcheted up dramatically.

All vehicles sold had a "condition report" (CR) that provided buyers detail about the vehicle before the auction. Online buyers began asking for more close-up photos of the scratch mentioned in the CR or a notation that the inside of the vehicle revealed the previous owner smoked cigars—all elements the person on site could see-touch-feel-and-smell.

However, the greatest change between online and in-lane buyers was the standards for arbitration. The old rules failed to take into account that the online buyer was making a purchase with only "at-a-distance" sight as their primary tool for gauging worth. To level the playing field the company instituted a "we'll buy it back" policy if the buyer registered any displeasure with the fairness of the deal within the first 30 days after purchase.

United Airlines could have taken a lesson from our auto auction client. Like a rattlesnake, Dave Carroll had given a noisy warning to United in the form of his clever video. It appears that United ignored the warning. Then, Dave struck and struck hard. He not only made three videos, he appeared on the CBS *Early Show*, CNN's *Situation Room*, and ABC's popular show *The View*.

DAVE CARROLL SPEAKS

"United has been in contact with me, and they have generously, but late, offered us compensation, and I'm grateful for that, but like I said before, I'm not looking for compensation."

The fact that Dave suggested they give their financial offer to charity could be interpreted to mean he was never asked: "Dave, what can we do to make it up to you?"

Had United responded immediately and appropriately to the first video, the sequel could have been a pro-United song and the emerging PR bite would have been prevented as the rattler slithered away. Had United monitored and used the power of multiple online channels, the situation could have been uncoiled and contained. But there was nothing about the video on the PR page of United's website. The unofficial "United Airlines Fans" site had nothing to say about it. And, despite the gazillion tweets, blogs, and posts about the incident, there were only a small handful of tweets from United, mostly outlining their offer to Dave.[14] Dave told us in an email, "I did say that if they were to make any commendable policy changes between then and my writing of song 3, that I would be inclined to be fair to them in the song. They never did throw me a bone to chew on."

The warp speed and surprise power of the Internet means the very best antidote to the bite of a wired customer intent on striking is to be a fast fixer and a sincere healer, not a sounding board. And, that means asking customers for their definition of fair and then adding to it. It means drawing the customer in as a source for learning, not reaching for the checkbook in hopes they will go away. Bottom line, it requires thinking of the Internet customer as a partner who, because of their access to many cyber villages, can be a valued scout, interpreter, and peacemaker.

Be Generous

Immediately following the first Dave Carroll video, the maker of his instrument, Taylor Guitars in El Cajon, California, featured Dave on their website along with his "United Breaks Guitars" video. They also contacted him and, in the words on their website, "offered to have our repair techs at the Taylor factory examine the guitar to see if there's any way we could restore its musical mojo."[15]

UNITED AIRLINES TWEET

As Dave asked, we donated $3,000 to charity and selected the Thelonius Monk Institute of Jazz 4 music education 4 kids.

When Delta Airlines lost a passenger's small caged dog, Paco, while it was waiting to be placed on a flight, Delta's spokesperson indicated that the best they could do was refund his $200 pet transportation fee, but only as a "credit" for future Delta travel. Of course, Paco's story went viral. The energy behind the story was less about the loss of a new puppy and more about the airline's miserly response. Delta later raised their atonement to $380 plus two more $200 vouchers. But, the rattlesnake had already struck!

What makes bigheartedness so potent on the Internet? We laud the speedy philanthropy of Taylor Guitars and scratch our heads at the penny-pinching orientation of the two airlines. Now, let's be completely fair. We do not know the content of the conversations between Paco's daddy and Delta or Dave's dialogues with United. Dave did tell us, "The donation of $3K to the Thelonius Monk Jazz School in my name was their decision and donation of choice." It's fairly easy to guess the tone, though. Dave launched a second and third video *after* hearing from United. Paco's daddy posted his Internet story (with photos) *after* getting Delta's "by the rulebook" offer.

Value in the Village

Social media like blogs, Facebook, and Twitter provide concrete evidence that customers are changing the way they define marketplace. In some ways the Internet is a return to the old-fashioned village. While the new village is a global community, it nevertheless has many of the features of the village of yesteryear. In a small town, merchants knew you and catered to your specific needs. They acted on history, patterns of previous purchases. They'd even open the store after hours if you needed something. Over the last fifty years commerce has become distant, impersonal, and one-size-fits-all as the service covenant has altered. The Internet in general and social media in particular have helped connect customers with businesses in ways that are more personalized, open, around-the-clock, and valued.

Another feature of the old fashioned village was generosity. The village is where the concept of "the baker's dozen" originated. Kids got a free taste at the candy shop; merchants gave away "secret recipes," and adults got a "take it home and try it" assurance behind products. There was no need for a written "money-back guarantee"—the merchant *was* the guarantee. The closeness of shared space required varied means to maintain relationship balance. Customers and merchants relied on neighborly practices. A spirit of abundance was a way to start and maintain valuable relationships.

Like the old-fashioned village, the Internet is a world under a microscope. Value must be real and look real. The eye candy of websites must be interesting, easy, fast, and imaginative, or the cyber traveler will only be a drive-by window shopper or a targeted bargain hunter with little intent of sticking around (called being sticky) or coming back. It makes generosity—providing *extra* to value, not thinking of value as *tit for tat*—an important means to ensure a genuine partnership.

Log on to Gerbers.com, and their home page is organized by the stages of a baby's life, from pregnancy to preschool. Not only are site visitors given product information relevant to a specific stage, but Gerber also provides information on growth and development, nutrition and feeding, and offers parental advice. At the other end of the spectrum, log on to Jackdaniels.com and, after putting in your birthday to get through the cyber front door, you are treated with a potpourri of recipes, stories, and entertaining trivia about Jack, Jack Daniels distillery, and Jack Daniels products. Intuit gives visitors smart advice by product and links them to a community of Intuit product users.

Applying the power of partnership can turn what might have become an Internet feeding frenzy into a happy ending. Earlier in the book we mentioned the Comcast customer who discovered a Comcast repairman asleep on the customer's couch. Using his phone, he taped a video of the scene. It seems the Comcast repairman dozed off while waiting for over an hour to speak with a Comcast operator. The video has been seen by more than 1.5 million people. The good news is that the wakeup call for Comcast triggered a massive and impressive turnaround.

According to Tina Waters, SVP for National Customer Operations, Comcast launched a company-wide effort to improve the customer experience that has included:

- Instituting a 30-day money-back guarantee on all services

- Giving new state-of-the-art tools and information to techs and service reps to lower service calls

- Implementing six ways customers could contact Comcast, including an email directly to the CEO

- Giving customers the ability to manage their Comcast account via the web any time of day

- Shortening appointment windows and adding appointment times that customers said were most convenient to them

- Creating a digital care team to engage customers via blogs, online forums, and Twitter

Go to

The late Geary Rummler was fond of saying, "You can take great people, highly trained and motivated, and put them in a lousy system and the system will win every time." We have included Tool #12 to help with processes or systems that are not helping to create a great service experience.

"Twitter has made Comcast more transparent and showed the benefit of listening to our customers through all communications changes," Frank Eliason, a former director of digital care at Comcast, told *USA-Today*.[16]

And, the result? A year after initiating the major effort, Comcast had already begun improving on J.D. Power scores.[17] The year the sleeping-tech incident went viral, the American Customer Satisfaction Index scored Comcast at 54. In 2010 their score had already jumped to 61! Listening, learning and adjusting are the never-ending lessons of the age of the Internet.

/\\/\\/\\

Internet is a word we repeat without thinking much about its real meaning. When we shorten the word to *Net* we remove the most important part. *Inter* means "between," as in interchange, interconnect, interface, interact, interdependence, and interpersonal. It implies mutuality and reciprocity, a give-and-take that respects both ends of a promise waiting to be kept. It can be the shining manifestation of partnership at its finest. And, it can transform a "wired and dangerous" customer into a wired and devoted one.

CHAPTER 11

Congruence
How to Get the Service Setting in Balance

Service "interior decorator" is a role every service providing organization should have. Businesses hire interior decorators to beautify their corporate headquarters. These professionals select the right paintings, the correct color for carpet and walls, the proper plants, and the best lighting to accentuate it all. But, who decorates the service experience in a fashion that brings tranquility to a customer?

A service experience is obviously far more than the customer's interaction with people, products and processes. Harvard Business Review defines it as: ". . . the internal and subjective response customers have to any direct or indirect contact with a company. It is all the details the customer experiences that determine the stories they tell neighbors."[1] Drive by a restaurant with a long line of people waiting to get in or see a marquee with a misspelled word and you have an impression. Open a bill from Acme Pyrotechnics or log on to www.armadillosunlimited.com and you are instantly flooded with sensory signals that tell a tale.

Customer tranquility comes in part when everything we experience about an organization, obvious or subliminal, fits. Should we, as customers, approach the organization with the slightest bit of uncertainty, anxiety, or angst, the sensory radar is turned way up for subtle clues that guide our feelings and direct our reactions. We can take the deep breath of serenity only when all seems right. We label this

THE CUSTOMER IS ALWAYS RIGHT!

B.Joo

"We've talked it over and we've decided that you must not really be a customer."

chapter "Congruence" because it captures the essence of "fit"—everything seems in sync with the intended service experience. Let's explore a simple but poignant example.

Miller Brothers, Ltd. is a men's clothing store in the upscale Buckhead section of Atlanta. They take creating customer calm to a whole new level. According to the store architect, Bill Edwards, "Owners Robby and Greg really listened to comments from their customers and we incorporated those ideas into the design and ambience of the space. The outcome is a well-heeled, clubby feel, with built-in clothing displays to blend with the architecture of the building."[2]

Imagine a men's clothing store with a large fireplace, hardwood floors, comfortable leather couches, a seating and eating area with TV viewing for sports buffs, plus a full-scale and upscale bar. "We wanted our store to be a great place to hang out and have a beer with the boys but also to be the best store in Atlanta. The goal was a place that was sophisticated, but fun," Robby Miller told us in an interview. "We care about customer comfort just as much as we care about the cut of a jacket or the superior quality of a dress shirt," added co-owner Greg Miller.

Their focus on creating a tranquil environment does not stop with design and decor. The entrance is a montage of live, colorful flowers. As soon as you walk in the front door, with or without a kid in tow, you cannot miss the table on your right, on which rests a large colorful gumball machine and a bowl of bright shiny pennies. The furniture has a worn, antique feel about it, as if it has been the nesting place for many, many lively conversations. The colors are rich and soothing, much like the inviting den of a rich country squire. You almost expect a fox hound to come through the side door.

The first person to greet you is a well-dressed clothier who smiles, nods, and speaks as if you are an old friend who has visited many times. "Welcome back. You know where we keep the good stuff." Even first-time visitors have little trouble locating the bar, should that be their inclination. There is no sales pressure. There is also no snooty look if you are there on a Saturday morning in your dingiest sneakers and most faded jeans.

Miller Brothers combines a seasonal trunk sale with low-country barbeque and brew. It's a memorable occasion. For example, they have not only invited folk hero University of Georgia football coach Vince Dooley to stage a book signing in the store, but they also held the late afternoon–early evening special event on the Wednesday before Father's Day.

Let's look a bit closer at the details of "congruence" offered by the example. Miller Brothers did not simply provide comfortable seating; they provided cushy, melt-into-the-cushions comfortable seating. Their restrooms are not simply clean, they engulf you in calm. The beer is not just cold; it is super icy cold, as if it had been pulled right out of a barrel of crushed ice. The bar is not stocked with second-rate whiskey, but exclusively with premium brands. Attention to comfort even extends to the potential little customer you might have in tow. Guess where Junior goes while daddy is trying on pants.

Now, before you rush in to the boss, claiming you need to add a bar to calm your customers, pay less attention to the particulars and more attention to the principles employed by Miller Brothers, Ltd.

Whatever your role in your organization, there are elements of that setting that you can replicate or influence. Getting congruence into the service covenant includes being an interior decorator for your part of the service setting. Consider these actions that Miller Brothers took:

- They went to school on the whims and wishes of their target customer.

- They paid attention to the details that send signals about the experience.

- They managed the choreography to ensure all parts in the service performance work together like a well-oiled machine.

- They made place, process, people, and performance work as a highly choreographed whole.

- They added simple surprises aligned with the experience they seek to create.

- They took out the clutter that clashes with their desired sensory experience.

- They made certain the set, script, and story (the scenography) worked together for a harmonious total.

Neuro-Linguistic Programming is a fancy but serious phrase coined by Richard Bandler and John Grinder for an approach to counseling communications.[3] They spent countless hours watching famous psychotherapists at work to discern the techniques they shared for putting patients so much at ease that they would reveal their darkest secrets or deepest fears. Among their learnings was the power of "matching and pacing." If the patient sat with legs crossed, so did the therapists. If the patient used visual language ("I see it as challenging"), or auditory language ("It sounds very tough"), or kinesthetic language ("It feels difficult"), the therapist adopted similar patterns that mirrored the patient's.

There is much more to the NLP approach, but its power lies in the creation of a deep rapport that comes from synchronization. Imagine if the NLP concept were applied to the service experience. The sight-smell-sound-taste-touch harmony would work as a whole. If you were in charge of an airport, consider the relief you could create for tired travelers if you used consistent, meaningful colors. Author Seth Godin adds: "Imagine how much easier it would be to find out where you were going if every sign with the word TAXI on it had it in yellow instead of white. Once you knew the color of where you were going, you'd just naturally scan for it."[4] That is congruence thinking!

Creating Tranquility Through Scenography

Flying from L.A. to Charlotte, Chip learned his seatmate was the re-nowned storyboard artist Tom Cranham. Tom's role as an illustrator was to read a screenplay, review photos of the planned movie set, and then illustrate the movie in cartoon-like style with a new drawing at each point the camera shot changed. The illustrator for such movies as *Jurassic Park, The River Wild,* and *True Lies,* he was en route to Wilm-ington, North Carolina to work with director Stephen King to shoot the horror movie *Maximum Overdrive.*

"Once I am on location," the passionate artist explained, "I will make adjustments based both on Stephen's review of my original drawings and what I learn about how the movie set actually looks." He leafed through a large drawing pad showing a collection of pictures. Some had the script or notes from the screenplay penciled at the bot-tom. "Once completed," he continued, "we make copies so everyone on the set—director, camera crew, sound technicians, and actors—can share the same vision of the end result."

A part of the goal of congruence is making sure everything in the service scene works well together. Take Stew Leonard's Dairy Store. The East Coast grocery chain holds a pile of records from a listing in the *Guinness Book of World Records* for sales per square foot, to *Fortune Magazine's* "100 Best Places to Work," to the Presidential Award for Entrepreneurial Excellence. From the staging of the entrance to the goofy characters wandering the store, to the corny music accompanying mechanical farm animals, to the tacky lines advertising their produce, the entire place is absolutely outrageous, and absolutely works! People, place, performance, and process are all intertwined and coordinated like the operation of a turn-of-the-century carousel. You enter the set and become a part of the set, not as a tourist watching an attraction, but as a partner with Stew, co-creating a wacky, wonderful, grocery-buying experience.

Scenography, the technical name for the work of the storyboard artist (or illustrator), originated in ancient Greece. Artists painted on stones colorful stage scenes for a theatrical production. Here, we use the concept as the strategy of integrating all the sensory elements of a service experience around a compelling service story or vision. The very best service providers in the world use scenography to craft a powerful experience for their customers.

We humans favor symmetry and balance. The concept of homeostasis (emotional stability) has long been a tenet of human psychology. Our psyche reads dissonance in an experience long before our logical mind comprehends a rationale. Far more than the urge to level a crooked picture or the recognition that something is off in a melody we hear, the dissonance arising from the absence of homeostasis even reaches to ideas out of alignment with our beliefs.

Creators of a service experience, once satisfied with the interpersonal or transactional encounter, too often consider their job mostly done. Little attention is given to what the customer's mind reads as out of sync. Even the couple enjoying that long-saved-for special evening at a swanky hotel senses symmetry and balance when they feel it, even if they can't detail exactly why. Scenography is the craft of making every component in the service experience "fit" with the promise made, or implied, by the value proposition of the service provider.

Vision

Service scenography starts with a clear service vision, or "experience picture," around which is crafted three crucial elements—script, set, and story. A service vision is a statement of the unique, signature experience an organization seeks to create for customers at every touch point. The Ritz-Carlton Hotel service vision was inspired by its namesake, The Ritz hotel in Paris. César Ritz in 1898 created The Ritz as the hotel fit for royalty. His intent was not just a physical structure that "enlivened the senses," but an experience that "anticipated even the unspoken needs of guests." The hotel is today one of the most prestigious luxury hotels in the world. Horst Schultz, president of the Ritz-Carton Hotel Company from 1988 until he retired in 2002, wrote that its service vision— "ladies and gentlemen serving ladies and gentlemen"—borrows in part from the original vision of César Ritz.

Script

The next component of service scenography is script. Script is more than the words spoken. It is the attitude or philosophy guiding all the interpersonal connections that reflect the service vision. It spans tone, attitude, non-verbal gestures, signage and signals used to communicate the language of the service vision. The Ritz-Carlton chooses the sounds of elegance and refinement: "My pleasure," "Certainly," or "May I escort you?" Associates send non-verbal messages to each other to signal a returning guest. Hotel signage is classy and unobtrusive. Associates practice assertive hosting with noticeable warmth and obvious attention to both detail and personalization.

Outback Western Wear in Magnolia, Texas, is famous for its wide selection of western gear, especially western boots. Western-wear fans in Texas take their boots very seriously, often spending a considerable amount of time getting a perfect fit, the right heel and toe, and the best-quality material, be it basic steer leather, or alligator, kangaroo, ostrich, or goat. A great fit requires trying on many pairs to find just the right one. At one time, Outback Western Wear customers being fitted for boots were asked "How about a cup of coffee or a soft drink?" The most common customer retort: "No thanks, but I could sure use a cold beer!"

The customers were really reflecting an attitude more than an actual request in their response—somehow the store's opening question did not go with the smell of leather, the sounds of the late George Jones, or the rodeo photos on the walls. Today the store starts the customer refreshment query with, "Can I get you a cold beer?" Sure enough, there is a large barrel of ice-cold beer in the store—not for sale, but for the refreshment of customers over twenty-one. Most customers opt for the coffee instead, but their reaction to the greeting question clearly telegraphs their delight. And, the inclusion of "the right beverage" makes the first impression congruent with the rest of the experience.

Set

Another component of service scenography is set. Set involves shepherding all the signals read by the customer's senses into a coherent whole. Those signals are to a service provider what stage props, decoration, lighting, and sound are to a play. Service set works when it is aligned with the service vision. Set is most effective when it enhances the experience without being the centerpiece of the experience. What that means is not that the set is necessarily understated; more that it is a near-perfect blend with all the other components.

Crucial to a great theatrical (a.k.a. service) experience is that the physical set is congruent with the vision. The Ritz-Carlton hotels select colors (cobalt blue, for example) found in luxurious castles. Lobby flowers look like rare foliage from the jungle, not ordinary blossoms from the local nursery. Thread count of sheets is as important as culinary perfection; artwork is as crucial as the elegance of staff uniforms.

Story

Story is the theme, the foundation of an alluring narrative, often complete with a backstory. The front or main story is what you see—a fantasy land commanded by a mouse (Disney theme parks), or, in Las Vegas, a trip to Treasure Island (Treasure Island Hotel), or a stroll through the streets of Paris (Paris Hotel) or Venice (The Venetian). A backstory, on the other hand, is sort of an amplified, embellished, exaggerated story behind the story. It can be important in enriching the story and giving service people a more profound understanding of its nuances or mythology.

The story at the Ritz-Carlton Hotels is all about the "warm, relaxed, yet refined ambience" found in a luxurious castle or an elegant inn. "Elegance without warmth is arrogance," Horst Schultz often says. "Our theme is the creation of an experience that enlivens the senses and instills well-being in our guests." Associates are schooled in the history of the Ritz-Carlton along with its core values. The backstory, known only to insiders and very special guests, includes secrets like the fact it was César Ritz who suggested Grand Marnier as the name for a liqueur created by his financier, Alexandre-Louis Marnier-Lapostolle, or the importance of the Gold Standard, 21st Day, and Line Up.

Every organization has a proud history or founding vision or unique mission to use as a backstory. Employees at FedEx all know the never-say-die attitude of founder Fred Smith and his struggles to start the company, building on a concept his Yale professor claimed was "interesting but unrealistic," that netted him a grade of "C." The story fuels the FedEx determination to get packages to customers no matter what. KFC employees know that founder Harland Sanders was given the honorary title of Kentucky Colonel in the 1930s by the governor of Kentucky in recognition of his contribution to the state's cuisine. Science Diet, a product of Hill's Pet Nutrition, traces its ancestry to Mark Morris, a veterinarian who, in 1943, saved "Buddy," the world's first Seeing Eye dog, from death by kidney failure, through a carefully crafted, diabetic diet.

Holographic customer service agents are now a part of the regular scene at the Manchester (UK) Airport. It could be a preview of coming attractions. Imagine a holographic person resourced with artificial intelligence and voice recognition. However, key to such technological advances is to ensure they fit. As appealing as Princess Leia might be as a modern art museum greeter, another character might be more in sync. [5]

Scenography is a critical success factor for service exemplars like Cabela's, Virgin Air, In and Out Burgers, and The Container Store. They understand that service is like theater—a performance in which all the parts must work together to create a special whole. But, unlike a performance that is witnessed from the audience, service is an experience that involves as it engages; includes as it presents. The more it envelopes the senses of the participant-customer in a manner that is emotionally symmetrical, the more it engraves in the customer the kind of peaceful memory that ensures loyalty.

Creating Tranquility Through Consistency

When it comes to service, consistency is not "the hobgoblin of little minds," as Ralph Waldo Emerson famously said. Customers require consistency for trust and confidence. Texas A&M researcher Leonard Berry found that the number-one attribute customers value in the service they receive is reliability, an organization's ability to provide what was promised, dependably and accurately.[6] Customers want the service from branch A to be as good as branch B's; they don't like having to choose a specific location—or a specific teller, floor salesperson, or waiter—because opting for others represents a roll of the dice. If every Big Mac was dependent on the whims of the cook assembling it, McDonald's would not be the successful brand it is worldwide.

Customers enter all service experiences with a set of expectations. They enjoy pleasant surprises, but there is a set of givens that must be present for the surprise to feel like a joyful experience rather than a practical joke. Southwest Airlines is famous for its comedy-loving flight attendants. But, let the aircraft encounter rough air and begin bouncing around, their hilarious one-liners will quickly turn into the language of a serious professional focused on safety. Humor in the air only works if passengers already feel safe and secure. You will never hear a flight attendant make the pilot the brunt of a joke or funny line. Passengers want to feel confident that the person up front is respected as a pro.

Consistency starts with having a clear understanding of what customers want to be predictable. Keeping a record of the subject of customer complaints can be a start. Asking for customer suggestions and feedback can keep you up-to-date on their requirements. Watching customers in action can also teach you a lot about their needs, expectations, issues, concerns, hopes, and aspirations. In Chapter 12, "Acumen," you will find a host of ways to better understand what customers expect and have experienced. What prompts an online chat with a call center rep? When customers ask questions of a service provider—directions, instructions, information—what typically prompts their queries? Are they lost, confused, or uninformed, and what does that teach you about what is important to customers?

Once you have a handle on customer expectations for consistency, turn it into a standard way of delivering service. Make certain the standard contributes to what you want to be known for by your customer. For instance, a hospital wanted to be known as the friendliest, neighbor-serving-neighbor hospital in the region. The nursing department concluded that too often patients stopped employees in the halls for directions. They painted various color stripes on the hall floors leading to a particular department. If a patient stopped an employee to ask "How do I find X-ray?" the stock answer was "Just follow the blue stripe." However, patients felt the new system, while efficient, was cold and impersonal—just the opposite of the hospital's service vision.

Ensure everyone impacting the service standard is clear on the expectation behind it. Collect evidence and feedback that let you know how well you are living the new standard in the eyes of your customers. Get a friend to take an empathy walk (be a customer) through your service process and provide you candid feedback about their experience and how well the standard was used.

Standards help create a consistency of experience that builds all-important customer trust. Whether promising package delivery "absolutely, positively" overnight, guaranteeing credit decisions on home mortgage applications within two days, or ensuring a response to customer phone calls within two hours, regularly living up to the service promise builds credibility and creates a bond with customers that becomes difficult to break.

When people know what to expect each and every time they do business with you (caring, knowledgeable and competent employees that won't let them walk away unhappy), they are more likely to return with their funds and friends in tow. But if you are seen as erratic and unpredictable—some days delivering on the service promise, other days treating standards as "nice" but not "need-to-achieve" performance goals—it creates a sense of unease and distrust that has a corrosive effect on loyalty.

Creating Tranquility Through Taking Out the Trash

"Take out the papers and the trash" were the opening lyrics of a song by the Coasters that spent weeks in 1958 as the number-one hit on the charts.[7] Many teenagers wore out their shoes jitterbugging to "Yakety Yak." The words hold a strong message for delivering great service.

All service has a certain amount of garbage. And, in a competitive world in which customers demand more value for their diminishing dollar, if you don't "take out the papers and the trash," as the words of the hit song suggest, you are not getting the "spendin' cash" you were hoping for.

Today's customer's higher expectations, shorter patience, and greater propensity to go elsewhere with their "cash" should be a wake-up call to ramp up close attention to service garbage, whatever hassles your customers. It means paperwork should be easier, processes should move faster, and every employee that customers encounter should be more helpful.

Organize a "service garbage patrol" to spot and report places where service is a hassle for customers. Some 2010 Convergys research found a strong relationship between effort and satisfaction. When a customer found an experience to be both satisfactory and effortless, they were three-and-a-half times more likely to say they were loyal.[8] It means the concept of "first-call resolution" may need to take a back seat to "first-contact resolution." Effectively addressing the customer's issue on the first call may not leave that customer happy if the call was made after not getting the issue resolved on the web plus not getting a response to an email. Garbage patrol includes integrating channels to effectively learn of customer hassles across silos, not just those within a silo.

Go to

Examining the entire context in which a service encounter occurs requires making certain everything works as a whole. A key part is a service vision, a clear description of the unique experience you want to create consistently for customers and colleagues. Tool #5 provides ways to craft that service vision.

Put your customer's earliest encounters with you under your service microscope, whether they be on the website, in the parking lot, or in the reception area. Are procedures and people user-friendly? Is it easy for customers to figure out where to go, who to see, and what to do? Examine all objects, forms, websites, or systems required for all service transactions. Are they clearly written, easily understood, comfortably navigable, and really necessary? The most precious commodity for most customers today is their time, and if you waste it by creating confusion or discomfort they probably won't come back for more.

Review your inbound call process. Is the system large enough and sophisticated enough to handle the call load, easy to understand and use, efficient, and time-effective? Do customers have 24/7 access? Can callers quickly and easily get to an operator if they desire and when they desire? If they must be transferred, how will it feel and sound on their end of the line? What do they experience when put on hold—silence, elevator music, or long waits? What is the garbage you need to take out?

Kill stupid rules. The American Customer Satisfaction Index (ACSI) selected TD Bank (formerly Commerce Bank in the United States) as the top bank in the financial service sector on the closely watched index. TD Bank created a "Kill a Stupid Rule" program. Any employee who spotted a rule that kept employees from wowing customers got a fifty-dollar reward.

Make it a tranquil day. Making service comfortable is all about making the experience calm, secure, and accessible. Customers should be able reach you easily whenever they want. What music could you play that could lower customer anxiety? Why not focus their experience on calm and comfort? Recall what your Realtor told you about getting your house ready for a showing—include fresh flowers and the smell of apple pie. Your customers deserve the same concept applied to your product or service.

/\/\\/\/

Customers today have a low tolerance for hassle. While they don't expect perfection all the time, they return to organizations that consistently demonstrate a commitment to taking the garbage out of service. Service comfort requires vigilance as well as caretaking. It calls for employees willing to raise their hand when they spot customer dissonance. It takes associates who see continuous process improvement as being just as vital as continuous revenue improvement. It requires people who make preventive maintenance an integral part of their stewardship of the organization's resources and reputation.

There seems to be a rise today in service garbage. As organizations cut costs, trim staff, and reduce trust in their customers, the byproduct is more "papers and trash" littering the service encounter and reducing calm. Take out the trash and your customers will reward you with their spendin' cash!

CHAPTER 12

Acumen

How to Keep the Customer Relationship in Balance

Adaptation is the catalyst to balance and tranquility. Relationships are always in motion. Successful ones adjust; unsuccessful ones rigidly polarize or just drift apart. In nature, feedback is the mechanism that makes adaptation possible. We call it the *acumen* of adaption.

Cows lie down long before a storm appears; cats disappear to a quiet corner. Dogs sense variations in barometric pressure, smell changes in the air, and know to get prepared for a tornado. Elephants feel the vibrations of an impending earthquake long before buildings start to topple. The 2004 tsunami that killed thousands of people in Asia killed few wild animals because of their early warning wisdom made possible by feedback. All these examples illustrate the capacity of animals to read environmental feedback in order to adapt and thrive.

Like the weather, customers are constantly changing. It takes feedback to adjust and thrive. The Internet has made the world smaller and faster, accelerating the change process. Today's fad quickly becomes tomorrow's antique. Without perpetually updated customer acumen, the covenant gets out of balance and we wake up one day surprised by how much the customer has changed—and we completely missed it! Amazon.com was surprised, for instance, when a computer hiccup on Friday night caused gay and lesbian books to be deemed pornographic and thus excluded from their offerings. By Monday morning Amazon. com got a wake-up call about the importance of monitoring customer

"It says they want our feedback."

feedback over the weekend. A few bloggers had mobilized thousands in protest.[1] Had Amazon had a way to rebalance the service covenant early Saturday, they could have completely avoided a PR barn burning.

Customer feedback comes in many forms. One type might be gained from examining history. Customer forensics teaches a lot of lessons from the past that can be beneficial in adjusting the present to keep a service covenant strong in the future. We will call this type of feedback "Something Old."

Real-time feedback ranges from simple devices like asking "What is one thing we could do to improve your experience?" to highly complex means of getting customer evaluation—their assessment of service performance. This is the type of information on which most organizations focus. The good news is it is current; the bad news is that it often can be misinterpreted if not examined with a larger context. We tag this type of feedback "Something New."

The third type of feedback is customer intelligence derived from a myriad of secondary sources. Reading an article about one of your customer's plans to downsize might change the tolerance you show for late payments. A study done by your industry association concerning the future of whatevers might suggest a more proactive stance on keeping customers informed. We label this type of feedback "Something Borrowed."

You already know where this is going! The last category is "Something Blue." This includes a careful examination of customer complaints and service breakdowns. It could also include asking frontline servers about the things customers seem most anxious about or require more than usual explanation about. All can be information that signals a change in customer requirements.

Something Old: Learning from Customer Forensics

There are many ways to use customer forensics. The Acme Company (obviously not their real name) uses customer forensics on lost customers, probing for reasons that might disclose lessons learned. When a large customer deserted Acme for a competitor, Acme "deputized" four employees to be service detectives. They sorted through records and interviewed customer contact people. They finally hit pay dirt when one of their security guards solved the mystery: when leaving one of their district offices the customer had complained that his last shipment containing time-sensitive material had arrived one day late, dramatically reducing its usefulness to the customer. So Acme added a question to their order-entry process that determined if "time of delivery" was merely important or absolutely critical. They also added security guards to their list of key sources of customer intelligence. Acme ultimately won back the lost customer.

We were assisting a large construction company with customer forensics on an important, and particularly difficult, customer who had yanked his business from the company in anger and frustration. One of the goals of the customer forensics effort was to equip our client with tools for future customer intelligence efforts. While sifting through correspondence between the departed customer and the construction company, their marketing director suddenly commented, "We have given this poor customer plenty of reasons to keep him up at night. This was a uniquely bad connection. If we had changed the connection early we could have changed everything."

The comment triggered a renewed look at the data—not as evidence of anger, but as examples of fear. Remember: anger is a secondary behavior and a cover for the fear underneath. The fresh interpretation prompted a deeper, richer understanding of the factors that signaled the customer that his construction project was in jeopardy. Without the project, his business was at high risk of bankruptcy. Without his business, his upwardly mobile wife would likely leave him. With a history of heart problems, such a chain reaction could threaten his life. Thus, his outbursts of anger were actually a cover for his fear-laden cries for help—all misinterpreted by the construction company as simply the grumblings of a high-maintenance customer.

Forensics help solve the mystery of a departed human; customer forensics help solve the mystery of a departed customer. Exits have many meanings. Some are legitimate churn, unrelated to service disappointments; some are at the receiving end of poor service. Unless it happens to be a case of "good riddance," deep understanding of the departure can help prevent loss of valued customers in the future.

Something New: Getting Real Feedback Real-Time

We are both fortunate to have been married a very long time. Like all important relationships, our respective marriages have had their ups and downs, leading us to seek opportunities for more than usual candor. The pace of managing dual, fast-paced professional careers with typical family challenges can work counter to the late-at-night, no-kid-gloves honesty we desire in our marriages.

A week-end couples retreat taken by one of us assigned the couple to write down the limitations each partner saw in the other and then read the list aloud. Such an exercise, done properly, can have a sobering effect. It created a new appreciation for Ted Levitt's *Harvard Business Review* article comparing a quality customer relationship with a marriage: "The sale consummates the courtship, at which point the marriage begins. The absence of candor reflects the decline of trust and the deterioration of the relationship."[2]

Getting real feedback real-time starts with viewing it like that marriage enrichment exercise—as a valuable tool for insight that can clear up potential blind spots and update understanding of the needs, expectations, issues, and hopes of the ever-changing customer. The means of input are many. Below are seven methods for getting input that we have found to be both simple and fruitful.

1. Scout Reports

Scouts see a lot, hear a lot, and know a lot. Yet they are probably the most under-utilized source of brilliance about what customers really value. Scouts are the frontline people who interact with customers ear-to-ear, face-to-face, or chat-to-chat. It is important for scouts to share their insights and stories about the good, the bad, and the ugly. Invite your organization's leaders to listen to customer phone calls or ride in the field with frontline servers with the intention of learning, not critiquing. Then, create a way for the collective learnings to move upstream to senior leaders, as well as into the hands of those who can provide a timely response. The more customers see improvement based on their input, the more they share. The more frontline employees are asked for their feedback, the more they listen to and learn from their customers.

2. Neighborhood Watch

Most employees are customers of their own company. As such, they can be a rich source of information about service experiences. Additionally, they talk with neighbors who vocalize praise and protests about the service they receive. This valuable conduit can be an abundant source of feedback. Employees with a company nametag can also serve as a channel for customer feedback simply by standing in the grocery-store line. Smart organizations create forums that enable employees to share their insights from these casual encounters.

3. Tapping the Customer's Sounding Board

John Longstreet, while general manager of the Harvey Hotel in Plano, Texas, held quarterly focus groups with the taxi drivers who frequently transported hotel guests to the airport after their stay. He knew his guests would more likely be candid with the taxi drivers than with the front-desk employee who routinely asked "How was your stay?" The mayor of Santa Clarita, California, holds an annual Hairdressers Luncheon to get input and feedback from people in a role most likely to hear what citizens really think and their suggestions for improving city service.

4. Up Close and Personal

Many companies have their leaders visit key customers. One company has its leaders visit the customers of their competitors! How do they get in the door? They refuse to turn the meeting into a selling encounter, positioning it instead as a forum to learn what their company lacks that their competitors seem to have. A major hospital had leaders periodically don the uniform of a frontline employee to serve customers personally. These face-to-face learnings are brought back to mahogany row to inform service improvement initiatives.

5. Fast Service, Slow Endings

Customers enjoy service that embodies a sense of agility. Our tolerance for waiting has been dramatically shortened by service providers who make delivery speed part of their core competence. However, customers do not like to feel rushed, especially at the end of their service experience. Ending call center calls with "Is there anything else I can help you with?" signals to the customer that the rep is watching call handle time. We all learned in communications classes what closed questions do to communications. By changing that sentence to an open-ended question ("What else can I help you with today?") not only alters the experience but it also opens the door for input and feedback while increasing the potential for first-call resolution.

6. Multi-Channel Response Systems

Make it easy to listen to customers by making it easy for customers to contact the organization through email, web-based text chat, toll-free numbers, and more. Many service-focused companies today have web-enabled call centers that route, queue, and prioritize incoming email from customers, enabling customer-service reps to handle email and real-time web requests just as efficiently as calls to their 800 numbers. Also, don't make trying to find an 800 number on your website like a game of "Where's Waldo?"

Many customers have a good reason for wanting to contact the organization via phone versus sending email or visiting the website's frequently asked questions (FAQ) page; either they can't find answers to their questions using those resources or they need more detail and nuance than those avenues provide. Zappos.com puts their phone number at the top of every single page of their website "Because," says founder and CEO Tony Hsieh, "we actually want to talk to our customers. And we staff our call center 24/7."[3] List your 800 number and email address boldly on every web page. Place large signs in every customer contact area with your toll-free number and email address in bold, and "beg" your customers to call, text, or email. How about a large billboard campaign reminding customers you really do take their input seriously and asking them to call?

7. Watch the Customer in Action

Customers often behave in ways very different than they predict. This implies that we must examine more than what they report in an interview or survey. Continuum, a Massachusetts-based consulting firm, was hired by Moen, Inc., to conduct customer research for use in the development of a new line of showerheads. Continuum felt the best way to really understand what customers wanted in a new showerhead wasn't to ask them via surveys but rather to *watch* them in action. According to *The New York Times*, the company got permission to film customers taking showers in their own homes (we just report this stuff) and used the findings in the new design. Among the insights gleaned were that people spent half their time in the shower with their eyes closed and 30 percent of their time avoiding water altogether. The insights contributed to the new Moen *Revolution* showerhead's becoming a bestseller.[4]

Something Borrowed: Connecting the Dots

A map confiscated from an enemy courier revealed the location of a system of shallow caves, each containing a cache of weapons used to re-supply enemy troops. However, when a wise Army lieutenant sent the captured map to a friend he knew could provide a deeper assessment of the terrain, he learned that each cave was located on a similar site—same type of soil, same topography, same elevation. Checking other areas like the cave sites produced another major discovery: there were many more caves not marked on the map that contained even larger collections of weapons.

The customer intelligence version of the captured map can be productive in unearthing valuable information about customers. The security guard's assessment of the demeanor of a departing key customer can sometimes be more instructive than forty focus groups and sixty surveys. Talking with a customer you lost last year might be more helpful than talking with the one you acquired last week.

Acquiring customer intelligence is an intentional effort to understand the customer. This search is typically combined with known socioeconomic, demographic, and psychographic data. With contemporary market-research tools, investigators can know the specific buying preferences of a particular zip code. Their forensic techniques can tell you what magazines customers read, the TV shows they watch, and what they name their pets. However, learning such facts is more like searching the caves marked on the map rather than discovering unmarked caves. Understanding customers requires the pursuit of wisdom and insight, not just the quest for information and knowledge.

Customer intelligence is different from market intelligence. Market intelligence teaches us about a segment or group and discerns how they are similar. Customer intelligence informs us about the individuals who make those buying decisions in that market. As you peruse car counts, per capita statistics, and economic projections, it is helpful to remember the words attributed to Neiman Marcus founder Stanley Marcus: "A market never bought a thing in my store, but a lot of customers came in and made me a rich man!"

Knowing what customers are really like starts with the recognition that reviewing the results from customer interviews, surveys, and focus groups is at best like looking in a rear-view mirror. Today's customers change too rapidly to rely solely on what they reported. Instead it is important to anticipate where they are going. In the words of one infantry captain, "Any military unit can figure out where their enemy is. Victory comes with figuring out where their enemy will be."

Something Blue: Customer Complaints Are Valuable Gifts

Just as personal relationships have their occasional rough spots, so too will a customer relationship have its ups and downs. If there's real long-term value in the relationship, both parties will have an incentive to overcome the periodic problems and, through doing so, make the relationship even stronger. In contrast, an absence of candor that causes one partner to gloss over or fail to mention problems reflects declining trust and a deteriorating relationship.

Avoiding complaints, pretending that everything is just peachy (even when you know it isn't), pretending to assertively solicit customer feedback on the one hand while backhanding the annoying customer for daring to utter a discouraging word on the other are sure signs that the relationship has not achieved enough maturity to weather the candor. That way lies dissolution.

> ### Go to
>
> Staying close to the customer requires never ending learning and update. Customers continually change. Tools #1, 6, and 14 provide extra help on useful ways to increase your customer acumen—focus groups, customer forensics, and surveys.

I'm Outta Here!

Accenture's Global Consumer Satisfaction Survey found that 69 percent of customers have voted with their feet in the past year, moving to a new provider for at least one product or service.[5]

There are four basic reasons why customers choose to vote with their feet, and go looking for another service provider rather than sticking around and trying to work the problem through with us: they don't know how to complain or have a way to do it; they don't want to be made wrong; they don't believe it will matter; and they worry about retaliation.

A strong, enduring customer service relationship will be founded on clear, open communications, whether the matter at hand is positive or negative. Customers who take the time to bring their problems to us, or offer advice on how we can get better at meeting their needs, are customers who believe we care enough to act on their complaints, not just feel good about their compliments. They're telling us they still see value in the relationship if, that is, things can get back to a sound and mutually satisfying level. They're really a golden asset.

/\/\/\/

Acumen means insight and wisdom. In today's changing customer world, it is acquired only through continual feedback and current intelligence. The pursuit of feedback serves many purposes. It communicates to employees that the customer is truly important; it telegraphs to the customer that their two-cents-worth really matters; and, for the organization, it keeps the service covenant in balance to maintain a healthy, positively memorable customer experience.

Acumen is a big word with a wide meaning. While the traditional definition is about being smart, it also means shrewdness. Its origin is the Latin word *acumere*, meaning "to sharpen." Bestselling author Stephen Covey listed one of his "7 Habits" as "Sharpen the Saw"—his label for continuous learning or, in his words, "the balancing and self-renewal of your resources."[6] Smart organizations find a myriad of ways to remain smart and shrewd about the ever-changing customer. Growing in a relationship—whether spouse, partner, customer or friend—is vital to growing the benefits of that relationship.

And now, we ride off into the sunset . . .

The main body of the book is concluding. What follows is an array of resources in a section we call "Flash Drive." Its intent is to bolster continual learning and renewal.

We hope this has been an insightful (make that an e-sightful!) journey and that the trip has renewed your allegiance to the nobility of service and nurtured your zeal to make customer experiences matter more.

In the face of data overload, cyber-sonic excess, and the grand-standing nature of cynicism, the route to healthy partnerships with customers can seem overwhelming if not impossible. But, we would encourage you to wear your customer challenges like an oyster wears a grain of sand. Be the master choreographer of the customer experience you create. Deliver over-the-top service from your heart, filled with the optimism of a child at the winter holidays as well as the unconditional acceptance of a loved pet. Let it be all about your customer, in word, deed, and symbol.

In this era of the Internet we desperately need partnerships—those neighbor-like relationships that honor service at a caring level. True partners remain loyal through good times and bad, through layoffs and lay-ups, through healthy moments and sickly madness, and through joyful wins and disappointing mistakes. Such relationship commitments start, and continue, with the expression of a partnership orientation: honesty, generosity, curiosity, integrity, balance, and an allegiance to collaboration.

The byproduct of customer partnerships is more than simply loyalty. The deeper consequence is that partnerships foster lives of peace, joy, and contribution. Partnership does not happen solely through good intentions. It starts with the courageous act to invest greater focus and energy on making service a cherished bond, not just an inconsequential business deal. And it starts with a single encounter—your next one.

PART THREE

Suggestions for Partnering with Customers

Flash Drive
Tools

Welcome to the *Wired and Dangerous* Flash Drive. That small device you plug into the USB port of your computer has two popular names, flash drive and jump drive. All three words—*flash, jump,* and *drive*—characterize today's "wired and dangerous" customers, so we thought Flash Drive a fitting label for the resource section of this book.

This segment offers an assortment of resources designed to help renew and rebuild the service covenant. Think of them as suggestions to help you stay wired to customers. The goal is a service experience energized by a spirit of partnership and grounded in a zeal to stay current on changing customer expectations. The more the customer experiences service performed in a partnership manner, even if the encounter is destined to be a single one, the more trust will be at the front door. The more the customer experiences a partnership tradition, the more likely they will return and become an advocate.

Plug this Flash Drive in your personal USB ("You Serving Better") port and benefit from the power and capacity of the resources here to enrich, encourage, and entertain.

This Flash Drive contains two types of resources:

- **Tools** are how-to instructions focused on a particular aspect of partnership effectiveness.

- **Favorites** are ideas to stimulate your imagination and continue your learning. Some Favorites are short essay-like items; some are lists and links.

Tool #1

For Calming Customer Crackpots, Bullies, and Militants

Southern politicians often have a homespun way of making a point. A few years ago a candidate in a small-town sheriff's election was overheard saying, "Criticize my drawl, you make me laugh; criticize my views, you make me listen; but, criticize my mama, and you're asking for a fight!"

Customer militants come in various forms. There are the customer crackpots with an ancient ax to grind, bullies only courageous on the "I can be anonymous" Internet, and radicals seeking a platform for some extreme point of view. When you or your organization becomes the target of their irreverent, inappropriate, and sometimes unfair poison, you can experience major mayhem from the way they shape opinion. Were this a real neighborhood, their views would be discounted as the babblings of a fool and carry zero credibility or influence. However, the concealment afforded by the Internet removes the capacity for character checking, so their toxic nuttiness, taken at face value, can do you real damage.

Sometimes the better part of valor is simply to ignore their caustic critique as too weird for comment. It can be a sign of great character to take the high ground and not glorify the drivel. But, remember, they step over a line when they "criticize your mama"!

John Kerry lost the presidential bid against George W. Bush, some say because he waited too late in the campaign to comment on the allegations of a group of highly resourced naysayers called the Swift Boat Veterans for Truth. The group of Vietnam vets, no doubt angered by Kerry's anti-war actions and testimony before Congress, claimed that 1Lt. Kerry was less of the battle hero than he claimed but was grandstanding and exaggerating. Some believed he played John Wayne on the battlefield solely to pad his resume as groundwork for someday running for public office. One such incident won him a Silver Star; however, his commanding officer joked that he had considered court marshalling Kerry for the event.

Kerry initially ignored the attack ads. By the time he finally spoke up, it was too late. The group had already tarnished beyond recovery his reputation as a man without integrity.

Decide where the "criticize your mama" line will be, but also how quickly the alarm bell will provoke action. Have a plan for responding. What erroneous, ill-founded comments will erode the integrity of your brand? What do you hear standing in the grocery line when others notice your company logo? Customers admire service providers who care enough about their organization's reputation to fight the good fight. You cannot remain silent. But, fight fiction with facts; meet hysteria with confidence. The more customers witness your passion rather than your anger, the more your intervention will be viewed as a mark of marketplace character, not as a defensive gesture aimed at trying to duck the spotlight.

Solicit friends and advocates to join in the fight with you. Never make assumptions about the motive of your opponent; this is not a battle of reason. Focus instead on what you stand for and offer concrete examples. In today's wired world, delay allows the viral effect to spread like an epidemic. Remember troubadour Dave Carroll? One hour in cyber-time is probably the equivalent of one month in snail-mail time. Speed of response is your friend in quelling the influence and reach of the adversary.

It may be appropriate to use multiple channels. A major snafu on JetBlue triggered emails and letters to key customers, ads in major newspapers, and TV appearances by senior leaders. Every public-relations channel available was used to quell the sobering effect of a group of "customers from hell" seeking to bring down the airline quickly over a major misstep on the Denver tarmac.

If there is a kernel of truth in the mean-spirited missive being fired at you, acknowledge it candidly and quickly. If some of the claims about Kerry had held a modicum of truth, he could have promptly stated, "I was a 26-year-old cocky lieutenant who wanted my share of the glory. However, there was nothing false about my being in harm's way in a heavily booby-trapped war zone regardless of the medals it yielded." He would have likely disarmed his opponents and been able to change the agenda from undeserved heroism in an unpopular war thirty-five years earlier to the present-day issues the campaign was supposed to be about. Candor and urgency are valued allies in the war against propaganda.

Tool #2

For Serving When Customer Pain Must Be Involved

Castor oil: "A foul tasting oil used in the 1950s to cure whatever ailment a kid claimed he had that would keep him from having to get on the early-morning school bus."

Chip's mother believed castor oil was a miracle cure. From a stomachache to sore legs to ringing ears, a spoon full of castor oil was the all-purpose answer to almost any malady. But, she added a small twist. Before she directed Chip "Open your mouth" she would ask "What is the best-tasting thing you have ever eaten?" For Chip it was wild blueberries. "Now, think about that great taste." Thinking about it never really turned the castor oil into blueberries, but it surely made it go down easier.

All customers face occasional foul-tasting aspects of getting service. Doctors have emergencies that leave you stranded forever in the reception area; airlines have cancelled flights; hotels have room keys that occasionally don't work; and popular restaurants have longer-than-normal waits at peak times. Smart service providers find ways to turn castor oil into champagne by helping their customers to "think about blueberries."

FIND A WAY TO BRING A SENSE OF JOY

When we exited the Hertz courtesy van at the Hartford airport, the below-freezing winter wind bit hard. But, the Hertz attendant had a warm smile and an eager-to-help attitude. "This is way too cold!" one of us commented. She almost giggled. "Now, you guys know, in Hartford we do weather as entertainment!" Ten miles down the road we were still laughing at her unexpected "wild blueberries" comment. What can you do to make service maladies seem more palatable to your customers?

Sometimes humor can send a message that "we don't take this seriously." Perish the thought! However, if there is a way to bring comic relief to an otherwise anxious moment, it can allay the pain and leave customers confident that they have a trusted partner at the helm. A Southwest Airlines plane made an especially hard landing in a cross wind as it came into the Harlingen, Texas, airport. As the jet raced down the runway passengers overheard the pilot over the intercom saying, "Whoa, big fellow, whoa!" His comical retort, as if he had accidently let passengers eavesdrop on cockpit chatter, caused every passenger on the plane to laugh. It completely erased the memory of the harder-than-normal landing.

LET CUSTOMERS "COUNT COWS"

Counting Cows was a backseat game that parents used years ago to quell the endless "Are we there yet?" queries from their children. The rules were simple: each person took one side of the car when the journey began. One point was given for every cow you saw on your side, five points for every horse, and if a graveyard appeared on your side, you lost all your points and had to start over again. Active participation in a simple, competitive game made the car trip seem much shorter.

Today's customers have a strong need for speed. They've seen faxes give way to emails, which gave way to text messages from anywhere at any time. Netflix and FedEx taught us you could get it next day; Zappos.com went even further: an order for new shoes placed online in the evening would arrive at our doorstep the next morning. Customers are as impatient and restless as youngsters on a long car trip.

But, there is a way to quell their annoyance with slow service. Let your customers "count cows"! Look for ways to help them put up with a delay. Just as Disney World entertains guests who are waiting in line to board that special ride, entertain your customers in an engaging yet appropriate way. Is there a way you can make getting service seem faster by turning the wait into a compelling game? How about a clever contest? A social gathering? How can you manage the customer's perception of service speed as you work to improve its reality?

USE FUTURE PERFECT THINKING

Think ahead and anticipate what might happen. This way you can proactively prepare the customer (or yourself!). A Northwest Airlines pilot took service matters into his own hands when trying to get a group of delayed customers from Minneapolis to Orlando on time. Because a mechanical wing problem had forced the already-late business travelers to get off one plane and trot across the terminal to board another, this pilot knew he was facing an angry, frustrated bunch of passengers. The new plane was only partly stocked and the pilot knew it would take another thirty minutes to finish loading the food and supplies.

So he made an executive decision: he stopped the loading of dinner and readied the plane for takeoff. Then, as they were taxiing down the runway, he told the passengers about his decision, saying he figured they'd rather get to their destination on time than have airplane food on the way. To make it up to them, he gave every passenger three free drink coupons to be used on the plane or anywhere in the Orlando airport. The flight arrived within twenty minutes of their scheduled arrival time. Not a single passenger complained about the lack of dinner inflight.

BE TOTALLY HONEST

Michael Graze had been looking forward to his birthday party. He and his mom had planned it out in great detail, inviting many of his school pals. So when the six-year-old's Power Rangers birthday cake from the local H-E-B grocery store arrived with Michael spelled "M-I-C-H-E-L-E" he was distraught. The great centerpiece of the party had turned to an object of derision through a spelling error! He swore he could never show his face in school again.

When H-E-B'er Julie McCoy heard of Michael's distress from his mother, she didn't hesitate. First, she was completely honest and took full accountability for the error. Knowing that apologies and refunds would be small solace for a little boy's crushed spirit, she arranged for a new cake and a new party—this one at a local children's amusement park, with Michael as host and H-E-B footing the bill.[1]

FINALLY, SHOW OFF YOUR BEST GENEROSITY

Special touches in times of worry make the Marriott Rivercenter in San Antonio a hotel customers love. A business traveler was awaiting the arrival of her husband and son for a weekend getaway after a long business conference. The two were delayed by severe weather in Dallas, which she happened to mention to a hotel staffer. To her surprise, the frontline staffer had milk and cookies sent to her room as soon as the two weary travelers finally arrived at 10 p.m. "That simple, unexpected, gesture of milk and cookies was a welcome surprise," she says. "It turned a very worrisome evening into a very pleasant memory."

All customer service has its "not so fun" parts. Great service comes from thinking about the customer experience through the lens of partnership. Stand in your customers' shoes and consider what would soothe anxious feelings. Be a strong steward of your customer's emotional bank account by depositing resourcefulness, patience, and generosity.

Tool #3

For Giving Great Lateral Service

If you asked a hundred people which African animals are the most efficient hunters, the most popular answer would be a pride of lions or some other member of the cat family. But, a pride of lions only captures their prey one in five attempts. The most efficient hunters are a pack of scrawny, painted wild dogs. Nearly 80 percent of their hunts end in a kill. What's the difference? They work as a true partnership just as you see in great lateral service.

Now, don't read too much into this metaphor by assuming we are comparing great service with efficient hunting. Just like great lateral service, it is the partnership wild dogs employ that is the crux of the learning. Lions only come together for a hunt, and then they fight one another for the spoils. Wild dogs share the rewards equally among pack members, including the injured or those too old to keep up; they even regurgitate meat for those that remained at the den during the hunt. Lions rely solely on instinct and brute strength in the hunt; the pride's actions are massed, not organized. Wild dog attacks are planned and closely coordinated, using techniques they teach their young.

Unless you operate a lemonade stand on the side of the road or are the sole proprietor of a firm, business, or practice, service gets to customers by way of a lateral process—somebody serves somebody who serves the customer. Unlike the signature, one-of-a-kind outcome a customer might get from a solo service artist, in lateral service the customer gets an equally precious result—the synergy of collective talents as enriching as watching the World Cup soccer finals or a performance of Cirque du Soleil. Service brought to you by a collective effort leaves you confident that your next experience will not be dependent on the turnout of a single person.

Great service requires great lateral service—the right hand caring about what the left hand is doing. It takes training and preparation. It requires taking care of the support people who may not be "at the hunt." Lateral service is the ultimate expression of superb partnerships; partnerships are *purposeful* relationships. Without partnership there is great risk of uneven, non-aligned service experiences. When customers are forced into picking a particular person, location or time to ensure they get the service they seek, because any other choice is a crapshoot, their trust erodes and loyalty fades.

PLAN FOR LATERAL SERVICE GREATNESS

"Hi, I'm Kelly. I'm on Elena's team. I have all your information in front of me. How may I help you, Chip?" These words started my second conversation with Dell after buying a computer from Elena.

We enjoy personalized treatment by service providers—people who know us. We even brag about our network. "Ask for Ted" or "Tell Susan I suggested you. . . ." Yet, there are pitfalls in relying on a single server. People resign, get sick, are transferred, and leave us floundering to start over with a new connection. But, it does not have to be that way.

Dell's Elena set it up from the beginning. "Chip, I want you to have my direct extension. But, if I am tied up with another customer, you'll always get one of my team members who will have all of your information. They'll let me know what they did to serve you."

MAKE YOUR PARTNERS SUCCESSFUL

We were working at the Ritz-Carlton in Naples, Florida. During breakfast we asked our very friendly wait staff what she liked most about working at the Ritz-Carlton Naples. Her answer surprised us. "Working here has made me a better wife and mother." Not willing to stop with such a profound answer, we probed a bit further and learned a lot about great lateral service. "At the Ritz-Carlton," she said, "it's not about me, me, me. It is about helping each other be as successful as we would like to be. It means stepping outside your personal chores to help out an associate. It means being kind and considerate; being patient with the little nits that might frustrate you and working together to make things go as smoothly as possible."

The world of hospitality, just like any other service-providing organization, has a front of the house and a back of the house. If the front desk clerk tells an early check-in guest that a room will be available at 2 p.m., but the housekeeper fails to get it ready as promised, the front desk clerk might take the heat but the brand or organization they both work for takes the hit!

CLARIFY PARTNERSHIP COVENANTS, NOT JUST OBJECTIVES

Great lateral service works because the relationships are anchored to a set of informal covenants or agreements specific to the relationship. "Successful partnerships are not built on deals and contracts," says Marriott CEO Bill Marriott, Jr. "They work because of the heart and soul of the relationship."[2] Partnerships are spawned from covenants that guide values and behavior, not just outcomes and results. Think about what most frustrates you about another person or unit you depend on to deliver service. No doubt they have a few sore spots as well. Ask them. Then outline agreements that, if kept, will short-circuit conflict and ensure smooth operation.

Talk openly about the appropriate reaction or recourse if a covenant is not kept. Keep communication lines open, even if the topic is an awkward one. Hold periodic "partnership check-ups" to explore what is working and not working and to discuss what covenants need to be added or changed. Just as a healthy marriage comes unraveled without dialogue about the relationship, so too will your partnership. Tension in the service relay is almost always obvious to customers, eroding their trust and confidence.

CREATE EARLY WARNING CUES

To repeat: partnerships are *purposeful* relationships. Success hangs on a perpetual focus on your mutual purpose or vision. Maintenance of the relationship—ensuring both sides feel valued and are receiving outcomes they seek—is as vital as your clarity of direction. Great partners establish "cues" or early warning mechanisms that signal hiccups in the relationship, allowing both sides to come together to address problems before they mushroom and damage a partnership beyond repair.

Every partnership experiences strain triggered by change, be it price changes, downsizing, acquisition, or uncontrollable factors like an economic downturn. Too often partners take the "see no evil" approach, ignoring intuitive signs of problems in the making. But in the best partnerships feedback is seen as nurturance (a kind of performance fertilizer) rather than critique; advice is valued as supportive instruction rather than a coercive expression of superiority. Cues serve as scouts on the lookout for hiccups in the making.

MAKE SILOS DISAPPEAR

Silos are the nemesis of customer loyalty. When partners aren't working as one to serve customers, when there are not seamless handoffs between internal departments in resolving customer complaints or if a spirit of cross-unit cooperation is lacking, it's the customer who often bears the brunt. Silos are eliminated by focusing on collective goals, not territorial gains, and by championing cooperation, not derisive competition. If there are conflicting goals, silo elimination will be completely impossible.

Partnerships are instruments of customer trust. They enable the kind of effective collaboration needed for seamless service experiences. They are the catalysts of alignment, that ingredient most crucial to service without drag, dissonance, or disappointment. Partnerships also require a deeper commitment than more transient service relationships. But they are almost always worth the extra effort. Not only are they more financially rewarding but they can also survive more mistakes, are more forgiving over time, and generate greater psychic payoffs than fleeting, more transaction-based business encounters.

BE THERE IN BODY AND SPIRIT

Great lateral service does not come from people who just show up to do a task. It emanates from people filled with spirit and animated to create results. The spirit leeches we spoke of earlier—those sleep-walking souls who keep one eye on the time clock and one hand on the exit door—are the arch enemy of lateral service.

We live in an era of spirit larceny. Downsizing has robbed colleagues of colleagues, leaving them hollow. Constant reorganizing has re-shuffled key alliances and stolen valued allegiances. The heartless hustle for razor thin margins has too often put short-term profits at center stage and long-term partnerships in the cheap seats. But, great service can come from the collective spirit of people who opt for optimism and work on the upbeat side. Again, show spirit leeches your joyful side and watch them disappear!

Tool #4

For Service Leadership in Turbulent Times

Great service can occur without great leadership. All organizations have those associates who work to give great service simply because they believe that customers deserve their very best. But it takes the guiding hand of effective leaders to ensure that great service happens consistently across an organization, and in a manner that supports the organization's quest for a good reputation, effective growth, and solid profits.

A point of caution: great service requires an organization that views its priorities from a similar perspective throughout the organization. When the leaders in one division have goals that conflict with the goals of the leaders in another division, it is often the customers who fall victim to the lack of alignment. Most organizations have end-to-end service processes that cross departmental boundaries, requiring synchronized handoffs. Without goal alignment, employees are left wondering why other departments seem to have little concern for delivering great service. The bottom line: align leaders' goals.

There are probably as many books on leadership as there are leaders! Most espouse similar truisms—walk the talk, hold people accountable, be clear about goals and roles, celebrate excellence, set a good example, develop others, and so on. We have chosen to highlight a few principles that best support helping employees rebalance the service covenant with customers. This is not an exhaustive list by any means. Consider them Chip and John's favorite tools for service leadership in turbulent times. While they are targeted at readers in leadership roles, the principles are relevant for everyone.

KEEP THE FLAME BURNING

People need a constant they can count on in times of massive change. That constant must be compelling and relevant; it has to be a foundation for everything. The flame most likely to evoke a sense of purpose or calling is an effective service vision, the picture of the unique service experience everyone needs to deliver consistently. The key to keeping the flame burning is to give every employee a match!

In his book *Stewardship*, author Peter Block states, "The traditional process is that management creates its vision and then the enrollment process begins. . . . Enrollment is soft-core colonialism, a subtle form of control through participation. Nothing has changed in the belief in control, consistency, and predictability, only the packaging is different."[3] It's not easy for leaders, conditioned to calling the shots and charged with charting the course, to embrace the concept of a truly shared vision, one that is crafted and renewed collectively. It requires involving everyone in the dialogue about mission and direction, and, more important, it means giving that input careful consideration.

KEEP IN TOUCH

"You can pretend to care, you cannot pretend to be there," wrote Texas Bix Bender in his book *Don't Squat With Yer Spurs On!*[4] Bender was describing a vital feature of leadership: command presence. People who spend more than twenty minutes in the military know the power of command presence. Officer school candidates are drilled on the power and practice of the manner of a leader—focused, attentive, and engaged. Command presence is not about control, it is about connection; it is not about power, it is about partnership. Leaders with command presence convey character.

Davy Crockett was a leader with command presence. "David Crockett seemed to be the leading spirit. He was everywhere," wrote Enrique Esparza, eyewitness to the Alamo, in a newspaper article following the legendary siege.[5] Great leaders focus on being there, everywhere, not in absentia. And, when they are there, they are *all* there—focused, attentive, and engaged. They hunt for genuine encounters. They also upset the pristine and proper by inviting vocal customers to meetings. They spend time in the field and on the floor where the action is lively, not in carefully contrived meetings where the action is limp. They thrive on keeping things genuine and vibrant.

KEEP OUT OF THE WAY

We use the phrase "keep out of the way" not as an invitation to hands-off abandonment, but rather as a caution never to use more leadership than is needed. If we have hired smart people and given them solid preparation and clear assignments, they shouldn't need a parent to watch over them. Limited leadership is the foundation of trust-building empowerment. Empowerment does not translate to *unlimited license* but rather *responsible freedom*. Effective leaders give servers the freedom to solve customer problems and answer questions on the spot within flexible guidelines. "To succeed with empowered customers," wrote Josh Bernoff and Ted Schadler in their book *Empowered*, "you must empower your employees to solve customer problems."[6]

Customers use the level of frontline empowerment as a peephole into the values of an organization. The more they witness or experience employees who act with authority on their behalf, the more their confidence in the organization soars. Empowerment also means helping people think like owners, coupling take-care-of-the-customer service with take-care-of-the-organization stewardship. That takes ensuring everyone has the most up-to-date information, the best training, and the kind of inclusion that helps employees feel like insiders, not like mercenaries.

KEEP RELATIONSHIPS EGALITARIAN

Power-free is the essence of effective partnership. Partner-leaders create relationships that are vision-centered, not power-centered. Partner leaders focus on support, not subservience; on commitment, not compliance. Partner leaders enlist employees as fellow alliance builders, working as equals for the greater good of creating loyal customers. This approach encourages employees to be partners with other employees, and it arms them with the confidence to exhibit partnering enlistment toward customers.

Egalitarian relationships are ego-less. The focus shifts from "all about me" to "all about us." Great partnering needs broad guidelines that provide "solution spaces" in which to operate. It takes knowing that mistakes won't be fatal; it relies on understanding that missteps in the pursuit of partnering with customers will be viewed as learning experiences, not handled with punitive measures.

KEEP THE FOCUS ON RESULTS, NOT ACTIVITY

Three turtles sat on a log at the edge of the swamp. One decided to jump in. How many are now on the log? Nope, there are still three. Deciding and doing are not the same thing. Until you execute, all decisions are just plain old intentions. Execution—putting skin in the game—is the true test of commitment. "I believe, I support, I approve" are all just weasel words unless they are demonstrated.

Working with senior leaders in major organizations who struggle with the arduous process of becoming more customer-centric, we are frequently reminded of what our mothers told us about "the road to hell." Creating a great, compelling service vision is important. Crafting clear, customer-focused service standards and norms is vital. Selecting people with a service attitude is major. Training people in ways to deliver great service (or how to effectively lead those who serve) is crucial. Determining the metrics and indicators of great service is imperative. But, in the end, all the planning and preparing is "just getting ready to." People judge your position by the one you take, not by the one you propose. Get off the log!

KEEP YOUR PROMISES

One feature that has been wrung out of the work world is trust. Trust is born out of authenticity. We trust others when we perceive their motives are unadulterated and credible. Think of the goal as realness-in-motion. Communicate your enthusiasm for the privilege of being of service to employees. Take a risk with employee relationships. Customer service researcher Leonard Berry has found that the attribute customers value most is reliability: "Can I trust you to do what you promise?"[7] However, trust doesn't begin with kept promises, it starts with a leap of faith! Someone takes a risk that builds experience, which leads to trust. And, when an organization takes a risk with employees and customers, employees and customers typically respond in kind. Then their loyalty soars.

Service leadership is about realness, not about role-ness. The stereotypical leader gets caught up with looking, sounding, and "acting" executive, and employees get a message of "plastic" power. Great leaders know humility bolsters trust. They are unimpressed with the trappings of supremacy and more interested in communicating an authentic spirit and an egalitarian style.

The trusting organization values generosity over miserly squeezing every dollar out of every transaction. This doesn't mean giving away the shop. Everyone in the organization should protect and grow the assets of the enterprise. However, customers remember organizations that refrain from nickel-and-diming them to death. That customer orientation is founded on how well employees are trusted by the leaders.

KEEP JELLY BEANS ON YOUR DESK

"Jelly beans" is our code word for the sense of fun today's employees desperately need. As customers aim their anxiety at the front line, employees need the bulletproof vest that can come from high self-esteem. Happy employees are resilient in times of chaos, courageous in moments of conflict. Sourcing an emotional strength that is bolstered by a supportive, affirming environment, they are able to absorb tension, converting it into compassion in arduous situations.

Be the ambassador of happy. Poke fun at yourself. Look for ways to shake up the place with quirky events, silly signs, and celebrative occasions. Constantly seek the means, moments, and methods to convey gratitude and encouragement for service greatness. "Thank you" are the two most important words in the English language. "Thank you" is not simply testimony to an occurrence but the conveyance of a feeling. It means communicating gratitude in a fashion that makes associates feel your authenticity.

You cannot give too many awards! Be accused of always being honest and genuine. Just because you happen to be leading the legal department or a group of super-serious accountants does not mean they are immune to a great belly laugh once in a while. Remember what William James said: "The deepest craving of human nature is the need to feel valued."[8]

So, there you have our favorites. Try them on for a while and watch the impact. Share them with other leaders and add new favorites. Remember: the number-one impact on customer relations is employee relations. As a leader, your influence, passion, and dedication to being the best you can be will go far in creating a leadership covenant that restores the kind of service covenant guaranteed to turn customers into advocates.

Tool #5

For Crafting a Really Cool Service Vision

Any good rancher knows that the task of moving a herd of cows requires bifocal vision. It is important to keep one eye on the cows immediately in front of you. Otherwise, an especially feisty steer can double back, costing you a lot of time getting the mutinous bovine back with the herd. However, it is equally important to have an eye on the destination. Without the long view, you risk moving the entire herd in the wrong direction, completely missing the gate in the distance.

Great service requires a focus on the tasks at hand (the customers right in front of you, so to speak). Equally important is a keen sense of the distant gate—the consistent distinctive service experience that makes a customer want to be a part of your herd. We called this long view a *service vision.* You will recall we earlier described the Ritz-Carlton's "Ladies and gentlemen serving ladies and gentlemen" as the service vision around which they align script, set, and story.

An effective service vision reflects a blend of four inputs: (1) customer loyalty drivers—those performance areas that have the biggest influence on customers' repurchase and advocacy intentions; (2) a clear-eyed review of the unit or organization's strengths, weaknesses, opportunities, and threats; (3) your own vision of what constitutes distinctive service; and (4) the active participation of all employees in the unit or organization.

So, how does a service vision help? It helps ensure the consistent service ("everybody singing from the same song sheet") that enhances customer trust. As customers, we feel more confident when there are service features on which we can always rely. A service vision makes those elements clear. A service vision can also provide guidelines for decision making. If your service vision focuses on being easy to do business with, it serves as an anchor in selecting approaches, practices, or procedures that enhance ease of service.

A SERVICE VISION IN ACTION

A clear vision is the mechanism that enables everyone's energies to be aligned toward great service. It is the tool that helps people make choices among initiatives competing for their time and budgetary resources. It also provides the underpinning for all service standards, norms, metrics, and structures. Service visions are best understood by way of example. We are very proud of our firm's service vision. It reads:

> The service vision of the CHIP BELL Group is to provide selected clients with relevant service wisdom that they experience as incredibly empowering and surprisingly simple delivered through a valued partnership.

Our service vision was crafted by focusing on the following key elements:

- *We identified our key customers.* For CBG, we are only interested in clients willing to give us tons of money for our services. *(Just kidding!)*

- *We identified the primary loyalty drivers for our key customers.* Clients told us they liked the manner in which we helped build client independence by teaching them how to do what we did for them. They also liked how low-maintenance we were to work with.

- *We decided what we wanted to be famous for in the eyes of our customers.* In other words, a service vision should have some "jump start" component that makes a unit or organization distinctive and exciting in the eyes of customers. Some of the features of the unique CBG Group experience include:

— Access that is easy, quick, and perpetual; response that is
stunning

— A consulting style that is generous, approachable, professional,
and slightly wild

— Practice methods that are creative, practical, and low-
maintenance

— Contributions that are cutting-edge and focused on client replica-
tion for success

— Client and associate dealings that would make even our
mamas smile!

STANDARDS BRING THE VISION TO LIFE

Service standards grow out of the service vision. They illustrate how
"the Acme Way" or "the IT Department Style" looks in thought and action everywhere—in the call center, on the sales floor, or in the check-
out line. Behaviors that consistently breed customer loyalty won't occur without standards and norms aligned with the service vision. Also,
service breakdowns often happen at the intersection of two internal
units that care only about their side of the equation. If there are precise, worked-out-in-advance standards about interdepartmental operations and cooperation, and if units are held accountable for meeting
them, you have a blueprint for efficient and effective execution.

The overall goal is consistent practice and aligned efforts. Such
consistency—delivering on promises, again and again—builds trust
in customers and helps cement their loyalty to the unit or organization. Service standards are the key eight or ten practices that are
crucial to making the service vision come true for customers.

WHERE DO STANDARDS COME FROM?

Addressing two questions can help develop more effective service
standards:

1. *What do customers value?* Begin by reviewing the primary
   customer loyalty drivers to ensure standards are built around

performance factors that customers really value, not those that have little impact on whether they decide to keep doing business with you.

2. *What is the organization's "special opportunity"?* Service standards bring to life the secret sauce that makes a unit or organization stand out from its competitors. Start by asking where the opportunities exist for differentiation in serving customers or colleagues.

A key component of the Chip Bell Group (CBG), a customer loyalty consulting firm, is to model great service to our clients. One aspect of great service is the ease of access and the speed of responsiveness. Therefore, one of the CBG standards is:

Access that is easy, quick and perpetual; response that is stunning.

TURNING STANDARDS INTO NORMS

While service standards are effective at establishing general guidelines and mindsets, they can be open to wide interpretation. The use of norms brings another layer of precision to the service vision by helping employees see what a standard looks like in action. Norms outline examples of behaviors and practices that demonstrate how the standard looks when applied in day-to-day service situations. Think of norms like this: if you shot a video of a colleague serving customers in a way consistent with a given standard, the resulting footage (the evidence) would be a norm.

Since the Chip Bell Group has easy access and amazing responsiveness as a key standard to illustrate the "surprisingly simple delivered through a valued partnership" part of the service vision, a key norm is:

Everyone in the firm is accessible by phone 24/7 unless in flight or with a client. Phone calls are returned within one hour; emails within three.

That means everyone in the firm is always on call. It also means everyone carries a cell phone and a means of getting emails all the time. This norm might be inappropriate for some organizations.

But, CBG's extreme accessibility is the means to ensuring that the response is stunning. "Surprisingly simple" in the service vision (the picture of the experience) becomes "easy, perpetual access" in the standard (the expectation) and "always have a cell phone and PDA" is the norm (or evidence) of the standard in action.

We believe three ingredients—dream, drive, and discipline—are required for the service greatness recipe. The dream (or service vision) must be aspirational, while providing a clear picture of the distinctive service experience the unit or organization seeks to consistently create, both internally and externally. The drive is the stick-to-itiveness needed to stay the course until new practices become everyday habits. The discipline means hardwiring standards (expectations) and norms (evidence) into the performance management process so there is both clarity and accountability.

Partnerships work when they have common goals, values, and purpose. Having a compelling service vision along with clear standards and norms ensures a payoff that can be powerful. Customers derive a consistency from which they draw trust. The unit or organization gains a means to ensure focus and rationale to polices, processes, and procedures.

Tool #6

For a Great Emotional Connection with Customers

Customers are favorably attracted to organizations when they get an emotional connection. This means heart-touching encounters filled with spirit, caring, and a positive attitude. Whether in line, online, or face to face, customers recall the experience long after they've forgotten you met their need. Here are eight ingredients for building customer loyalty through emotional connections.

1. Be the Attitude You Want Your Customers to Show

We all enjoy serving happy customers. You can help them act pleasant by showing them how. Aim your best smile and warmest attitude toward your customer. Then, deliver a warm greeting that says: "I can't wait to give you really great customer service." Optimism and joy are contagious.

2. Never Let Customers Leave Disappointed

Even if you can't always give customers what they want, you can always give them a great service experience. Find a way to help. Make sure they leave remembering your great smile and upbeat disposition.

3. "The Answer Is Yes. Now, What's Your Question?"

This "we'll figure out a way to do whatever you need" tells customers your organization has a *can do* attitude. Go out of your way to help. Show customers your pride. Try to never say no to customers unless their requests are inappropriate or unethical.

4. Great Manners Make Customers Loyal

Customers enjoy getting respect and manners. Customers may not always be right, but they are always the customer. If they all decided to not return, you'd be out of a job!

5. Listen to Learn, Not to Make a Point

One challenge we both had as parents was listening with no agenda. When our children expressed any concern, we'd feel the need to make a point, teach a lesson, or offer advice. Most parents have that challenge. When we stopped trying to be smart daddies and simply listened, our kids began to trust us because they felt heard and valued. Customers are the same; give them your undivided attention.

6. Find Customers, Don't Make Them Find You

Staff costs can be the most expensive item in the company budget. It can sometimes mean too many customers for the number of people to serve them. It also means being more assertive in finding customers to serve. Never let customers have to search for assistance. And, let your "How may I help you?" sound like you mean it.

7. Fix the Customer, Not Just the Customer's Problem

It is not enough to fix a customer's problem when things go wrong. Just as important is fixing the customer's feelings. Give customers a sincere apology, show you understand their concern, and let them see how fast you are working to get them back to normal. Follow up after their disappointment to make sure they are okay.

8. Thank Customers Like You Really Mean it

Customers love it when you tell them you appreciate their business. They never forget they have options and they feel valued when you show you never forget that either. Sound enthusiastic! If you sound like a "thank-you-for-shopping-at-J-Mart" robot, they will remember your insincerity, not your gratitude. Be a joy carrier. If you give customers the best that you have, the best will come back to you!

Tool #7

For Conducting a Truly Focused Focus Group

A focus group is literally a group conversation with a singular focus. Skilled focus group leaders clarify the interview intent, outline the protocols, and facilitate the discussion to yield an open and comfortable forum for beliefs, issues, and assessments. When a focus group is conducted properly, each participant feels their say was as valid as all others. With proper guidance, the conversation can feel as if attendees are collectively involved in a treasure hunt to unearth choice nuggets of customer intelligence to be later refined.

WHY CONDUCT A FOCUS GROUP

Focus groups are qualitative research tools designed to do what quantitative research (like a survey) cannot do. While quantitative research is by nature more scientific and statistically valid, it cannot provide the depth of understanding yielded by a conversation with a purpose. It's not that focus groups are superior to other data-gathering methods, they simply serve a different purpose. As a key action-research method, focus groups are used to spot themes, trends, and issues in a fashion often missed by the typical customer survey. The focus group is primarily a tool for general direction finding, not precise decision making. If six customers in a focus group (out of a thousand total customers) say your reception area is too cold, it might cause you to ask others about the temperature. You would not automatically make a temperature change based on the input of a few people.

Focus groups lend color and description to issues that can only be mentioned in a survey. If a researcher were to design a survey that would yield as much information as a focus group, no one would complete the survey—given the length it would need to be. However, if you asked customers about your website on a survey and their most common answer was "not very good" or "too slow," it would leave you with the accurate view that there was dissatisfaction with the website, but little information about why or how the website might be improved.

WHOM TO INVITE

Great focus groups start with having the right people. Eight to ten people provides enough diversity for interest and rich discussion yet is not so large that participants have limited time to air their views. The "right" people includes participants who are:

- *Experienced.* Make sure attendees have had recent experience with whatever the focus of the focus group happens to be.

- *Diverse.* Make certain attendees are not all alike. The more diverse the group, the better. The ultimate goal is to have the composition of the group be very similar to the composition of the entire target population.

- *Non-controversial participants.* This does not mean you want attendees with only plain vanilla views. It does mean eliminating participants you know have a major personal issue and may use this forum to dominate, exert undue influence, and otherwise use it as a bully platform.

- *Wild cards.* Sometimes there is merit in having a unique participant. This might be someone who can help bring a sense of optimism, or humor, or history to the focus group session.

HOW TO START

First, be a host. As participants arrive, welcome them and thank them for attending. Once all have arrived and are seated around a conference table (or in a circle, if no table is available), welcome them to the focus group.

- State the purpose of the session.

- Let participants know who you are.

- Tell participants the ground rules.

- Ask participants to introduce themselves and state their role (or some connection to the setting or your organization).

- Introduce your note taker. If you are leading the focus group by yourself, have someone from your unit take notes. It is just too hard to lead, listen, and write at the same time.

- Ask the first question.

- Listen to learn.

- Listen like you are at a raffle.

- Look like you are listening.

- At the end, thank participants for coming and let them know what will happen with their input. Never make promises you cannot keep.

- Have the notes typed quickly before the details fade.

Think of a focus group as the modern-day version of a chat around the campfire; it can be a spirited assortment of fact and opinion, rumor and myth. However, out of this forum can emerge a blend of insights that reflects real people talking about real issues in a real way. Properly managed and interpreted, the results are a valuable way to supplement quantitative research for better understanding what your customers think.

Tool #8

For Serving as an Expert

It all started in a discussion with a start-up company about how customers assess the performance quality of a service skill they know nothing or little about. The particular performance happened to concern an auto mechanic.

As patients, we are all gifted at assessing the excellence of our surgeon's bedside manner. But how do we gauge the quality of what the surgeon did "under the hood"? Obviously, not with the perspective a fellow performer might have—another surgeon can judge surgery quality with a lens unavailable to the customer on the receiving end of the scalpel. So, what are the signals "novice" customers can use to bolster confidence in the non-bedside manner part of any expert?

Chip recently had a tooth capped. The procedure was as smooth as newly polished enamel and he cheerfully wrote Dr. Norman Lee a check for a grand. With the experience fresh in mind, we reflected on the features of that experience as we worked with our mechanic-shop client. Dr. Lee established rapport filled with respect, narrated his procedure, spoke in "smart adult," showed Chip the "busted parts," and created a pleasant ending. Whether it is a doctor, dentist, mechanic, or Mr. Stereo Wizard, serving from the position of expert requires special tactics.

ESTABLISH A RESPECT-FULL RAPPORT

Imagine looking in your rear view mirror only to see the flashing lights of a police cruiser. Glancing at your speedometer, you realize you are driving 15 mph over the clearly posted speed limit. You pull over, remove your driver's license and insurance card, hand over your documents, and wait for the officer's opening line. But, what if the officer respectfully asks: "Mr. Jones, is there an emergency I should know about?" Instead of a tone of judgment you get a big helping of genuine concern. Even if there is a speeding ticket at the end of the encounter, your memory of it will be completely different than if the transaction had started with: "Mr. Jones, do you know how fast you were driving?"

Dr. Lee begins his dental wizardry by briefly reconnecting from the last visit, chit-chatting about non-dental topics, and then asking a few basic diagnostic questions. Most important, he does it all sitting eye-to-eye with his hands in his lap, not in your mouth. Despite his being north of sixty-five years old, he addresses his patients with "sir" and "ma'am." More than simply a Southern tradition, he creates a respectful partnership, not a condescending patient-ship.

NARRATE THE SERVICE PROCESS

Dr. Lee narrates the dental procedure, sparing no detail about what he does at each step and why. You get the experience a new dental student might get, learning from a pro. His "lessons" reflect a passion for dentistry and an excitement about getting to work *with* his patient, not *on* his patient.

John recently had a close encounter of the power outage kind. He called Georgia Power and, within minutes, got Greg, the master trouble man. Anxiety started to lift when Greg exited his truck and exclaimed: "I remember this house and those two great dogs!" Power and trust were restored when Greg analyzed the situation, detailed to John the electrical diagnosis and repair procedure, provided updates during restoration, and then briefed John on all the what's and why's before boarding his truck to chase other power outage demons. John and his family now speak of Greg as if he was their very own personal power expert.

We were on a Delta flight to Dallas. As we were ready to depart, the captain announced a mechanical problem in need of repair before pushback. Attentive to the reaction of passengers when delays are involved, we watched their initial anger plummet during the one-hour delay as the captain came on the intercom every few minutes to provide us a detailed update on the progress of the repair. We were fortunate to be sitting near the front of the plane. Every time a mechanic left the cockpit the pilot immediately shared his latest briefing with passengers. By the time the plane backed away from the gate, passengers were calm and peaceful.

SPEAK IN "SMART ADULT"

Experts often love their technical jargon—especially that which reminds everyone in earshot that they are indeed authorities. You

sometimes get the sense all their self-esteem is wired to their knowledge, and if they were to share it with others they would no longer
be needed. Also smart-alecky are nurses who assume every patient is
a hearing-impaired idiot! They rely on robotic patronizing ("It's time
to take *our* medicine") and use unwelcome, sugar-coated familiarities
("Sweetie," "Honey") to entice their patient to cooperate.

Dr. Lee speaks in "smart adult." He assumes patients under his care
are intelligent, and capable of following a semi-technical explanation of what is happening in their mouth. The airline pilot bolstered
passenger confidence even while using some aeronautics lingo we
did not understand. The key is to let a respectful attitude permeate
the interchange. If expert servers strip out all the jargon, customers might question their expertise, but if the dialogue is *all* jargon,
customers will doubt sincere interest in their understanding and
learning.

SHOW THE BUSTED PARTS

John's favorite auto mechanic always shows the damaged or malfunctioning parts after he meets John in the waiting room following
car surgery. The practice does more than reinforce a trust-building
perspective that only necessary work was performed. It demonstrates an allegiance to customer education and the growth of a
fully informed partner. Dr. Lee periodically pauses during a dental
procedure to grab the hand mirror and let the patient observe the
progress.

Direct Connection Computer Services in Dallas, Texas, specializes in
advanced computer networking and repair. Take a computer in for
quick repair and you just might be invited back to the technicians'
work area. "Some of our customers are so emotionally attached to
their laptops, they feel queasy watching the tech take them back,"
says owner Fred Givhan. "We've even made it a practice with our
more experienced customers of getting them involved in the repair
if they wish. Even if it's holding a wrench for the tech, sometimes
involvement helps allay their anxiety. Besides, they learn a lot about

the internal workings of their computer if they get to observe the 'surgery.'"

CREATE PLEASANT ENDINGS

Great beginnings require the emotional bookend of a great ending. Product manufacturers are object makers; service providers are memory makers. The way the service experience ends can be a key part of a pleasant memory. Dr. Lee always ends his "fix-something" procedure by sitting back in a chair, summarizing his work, answering questions, and planning the next visit. There is typically a follow-up call the next day to make certain all is well and that patient memories are still pleasant.

Order personalized award ribbons from the Award Company of America in Tuscaloosa, Alabama, and your order comes with a thank-you note that contains the words "I am the machine operator who actually made your ribbons. I am very proud of my work. We want to give you personal service. If you are dissatisfied for any reason, please contact our customer service department. They will contact me and I will personally correct any problem. Thank you for your order. We look forward to receiving your next order." If you order personalized items from StitchAmerica.com in Bremen, Georgia, you get an email as soon as your order ships. But, here's the best part. You get another email indicating when your order arrived and who signed for it!

The future of customer service will be characterized in part by a stronger and more pervasive reliance on experts. The sheer complexity of work and life will make do-it-yourself rare. Service providers in the business of delivering expertise along with bedside manner will be tempted to tout their special competence by keeping customers in a dependent mode. Smart experts will be those who embrace a partnership philosophy, inviting the customer into a collaboration that enriches the service experience while underscoring the special proficiency.

Tool #9

For "Serving in the Dark" Like a Partner

How do you create a partner-like relationship with customers whose faces you never see? There have always been a host of service providers whose only service signature was the quality of the work they left for the customer—the hotel housekeeper, the auto repair person on the other side of the "customers not allowed beyond this point" sign, and the night nurse who checks your medical stats after major surgery when you are too drugged to communicate. But what do "serve in the dark" providers do to create a solid interpersonal relationship with customers?

The route to creating a positive service relationship with customers receiving service without direct contact is to simulate the quality of a partnership. As with service in general, the effective management of service details can turn an "at arm's length" encounter into a responsive, kinship experience. It means first making the relationship matter and then seeking subtle but powerful actions to communicate care, trust, and authenticity.

On a three-week driving vacation, a couple stopped at a coin-operated laundry in Montana. It was very early in the morning. The place was spotless, inside and out. And empty.

A pot of hot coffee and a vase of fresh flowers rested on a small wooden table next to the change machine. Two snapshots of the owner's family adorned the bulletin board, along with a 24/7 phone number "if we can help." Other customers had accepted the obvious invitation to add pictures of their families. On the wall was a colorful welcome sign, including a reminder: "Don't forget we have free wi-fi." The newspaper rack had an unexpected surprise—a left-behind *Wall Street Journal*. And, it was that day's edition! The couple felt as welcome as the previous customers whose photos were on the bulletin board.

USE THE POWER OF SIGHTS, SIGNALS, AND SYMBOLS

That coin-operated laundry offered more than a functional transaction. It provided a cavalcade of communications designed to send a clear set of messages—you matter, you are not alone, and you are welcome. All sense of separation had been removed from the experience.

Look at all the sensory signals and symbols around you. Do signs or website banners sound like warm instructions to valuable partners, or like tough laws for greedy criminals? Like the library that changed "overdue fines" to "extended-use fees," the tone can communicate a lot to your customers. "Don't leave trash on the floor" can be altered to read "Thank you for helping us keep your laundromat as clean as you want your clothes to be." "Our washers are allergic to liquid Clorox" has a completely different feel from a "Thou shalt not. . . ."

Find a way to leave behind personalized communication to frequent customers. Chip orders his dress pants from M.L. Leddy's, an upscale western-wear store in the historic Stockyards section of Fort Worth. John Ripps is the sales rep he emails but never sees. Chip's pants measurements are on file; he simply requests cloth swatches, selects one or two and places his order with John. Two days after any purchase Chip gets a handwritten thank you note. When the tailored pants are made, he gets a heads-up email (or phone call) from John: "Partner, your pants are being shipped to you today and they are truly gorgeous!"

ALWAYS PROVIDE A BACK DOOR

Customers enjoy the convenience of print-at-home tickets, online shopping, online reservations, and so on. They like automation if it works, was crafted with them in mind, and makes their service experience easy. They prefer fast, simple, and *their* way. *Channel* means a medium of transmission. If the transmission feels one-way to the customer, they can feel as alone as the vending machine user in an isolated location.

Customers also want to be able to connect quickly and easily with a human being to bring fast resolution to their problem. We have described some great web-based companies that practically scream "We would love to talk with you if you need us!" Partnering in the dark means creating an experience that feels as if there is a guardian always watching over the encounter, eager and able to help if there is a hint of consternation by the customer.

The best websites are easily tailorable by customers with obvious access to "somebody back there" via numerous channels—"call us, web chat with us, email us, Pony Express us." The message should be "We are here for you and enjoy communicating." Ensure all customer-contact people have easy access to customer information. At USAA every phone rep has instant access to all customer files, including the customer letter that arrived this morning.

TRUST YOUR CUSTOMERS

Bob Frandsen of Homestyle Laundries says, "One thing I do to keep customers loyal is that I always send out the customers their refund money if they have filled out a refund slip. Even if they put down that they only lost 25 cents, I spend 44 cents in postage to send them their refund." Trust your customers and they will trust you back.

We are both fans of Dell Computer. Should your newest laptop computer have a gremlin inside, Dell will send the replacement computer along with a box to return the sick computer—not the other way around! They trust their self-service customers, even with a pricey laptop.

Airport concession stores sometimes put the morning newspaper purchase on the honor system. Instead of standing in line just to buy a *USA Today*, customers pick up a copy as they put a dollar through the slot in the money container above the papers. When store operators are asked about the end-of-the-day shrinkage, they will tell you that, while they may lose a paper or two, it is more often due to custom-

ers' accidently picking up two copies instead of one. The trust practice benefits the in-a-hurry customer trying to catch a flight. And, it
helps the store to manage efficient traffic flow with customers buying
either more items or items less common than a newspaper.

John is crazy about his Kindle. He will tell you that he reads more
now than ever! Amazon.com has made choosing books an amaz-
ingly easy and user-friendly process. Yes, as everyone knows, their
web site recommends new books for him and he can see what other
readers have to say about them. What he likes most is the ability to
download a book "appetizer" and, if he enjoys the appetizer, point
and click from his Kindle to have the entire book downloaded in seconds. It seems magical, and very personal!

"Serving in the dark" does not have to be silent service, stoically
given without customer rapport. The superior service provider finds
ways to build a partnership with self-service customers even if that
relationship must be more like one with a dedicated pen pal than
a friendly neighbor. As customers require service delivered more
quickly, more independently, and with greater convenience than
ever before, "serving in the dark" will become, to paraphrase the
ad line, "the next best thing to being there."

Tool #10
For Firing a Customer

We all know customers are not always right, whether it's behavior that
oversteps the bounds of civility, invalid claims, unreasonable demands,
or out-and-out error or misjudgment. But, owing to their status as the
lifeblood of any organization, customers are always worthy of fair and
considerate treatment. They are always *the customer*. Wise units
and organizations focus on helping customers "discover" an error or
misconception on their own rather than rubbing their noses in it.

There will come a time, however, when it is appropriate to consider firing a customer. When the emotional or economic toll exacted from serving continually abusive or extremely high-maintenance, low-profit customers starts to outweigh the return on the investment, it is time for a customer exit strategy.

WHEN TO TELL A CUSTOMER TO "HIT THE ROAD"

In addition to worries about replacing lost revenue, the negative word of mouth we fear they will spread as a result of being fired often keeps us from lowering the boom on highly toxic or bottom-line eroding customers. And, in the viral world, the word-of-mouth concern should definitely be part of the decision-making process. However, keep in mind that our projections usually prove to be far worse in our imaginations than in reality. People pay closest attention to word of mouth they perceive as credible and coming from a reliable source. The desperately-in-need-of-firing customer more often than not is seen by others as a perpetual victim and corrosive influence; consequently, their tales of woe and great injustice are often discounted by friends, colleagues, and even family.

The challenge, of course, is deciding at what point the rewards of being without the customer outweigh the potential consequences of firing him or her. It helps to remember that the payoff from customer firings won't necessarily be financial—at least not right away. The real dollar payoff comes when you replace that fired customer with one who's far easier to do business with, and who doesn't drain your organization of emotional, time, or monetary resources.

THREE REASONS TO CONSIDER FIRING CUSTOMERS

Customers should be encouraged to exit for one of three reasons: they're costing you too much financially, they're taking too much of an emotional toll, or they're violating a key value of your organization.

The financial cost means profit—most organizations are, after all, in business to ensure that revenues adequately exceed expenses.

Not always at the outset, but over time. With advertising, marketing, sales, and solicitation expenses, there's always a "sunk cost" in acquiring customers. If there's not sufficient return on that initial investment over time, you'll want to rethink whether a continued relationship makes sense. Where you draw the line depends on your own tolerance for red ink. Without a compelling reason to be tolerant, we'd suggest you have none.

The emotional costs involve the wear and tear on frontline associates. Some customers are so taxing or abusive that the damage they do to employee self-esteem or everyday resilience robs you of the enthusiasm to effectively serve other more deserving or valuable customers. Have you witnessed repeated abuse of frontline people by this customer? If yes, it may be time to consider favoring frontline morale over a given customer's revenue contribution.

The final reason to bid customers adieu is the clear violation of a key organizational value. This travels beyond morality or ethics infractions (the consequences for such violations are often cut-and-dried) to more nebulous values-based scenarios. If your reputation is built on responsiveness and you have a customer whose chronic demands for special attention are causing serious delays in your operation, it might warrant parting ways.

Whatever the conditions, make sure you've exhausted all reasonable options before cutting the customer cord. In some cases you'll find special efforts can still "save" profitable but difficult customers on the verge of being fired.

THE FIRING ACT: DO'S AND DON'TS

Firing a customer is a bit like disarming a bomb; "very carefully" is the operative term. The goal is to subdue animosity without scattering aftermath. Sometimes customers are so incensed at losing a favorite punching bag—even though it's actually you who's "lost" them—they can move quickly from anger to vindictiveness, seeking opportunities to punish, not just put down. You can limit your chance of such backlash by handling firings in cool-headed but still sensitive ways.

WHEN FIRING FOR ECONOMIC REASONS

Firing for economic or bottom-line cause should always be rational, never emotional. Rational firings are laced with up-front motives and clearly spoken rationales, with an emphasis on how a continued relationship will negatively affect the business, not on how a parting of ways will make your long-suffering staff feel like it's just won the lottery. "Mr. Jones, we've greatly appreciated your business for the last year. We have elected to apply our limited resources in a new direction and will not be soliciting your business in the near future. Should you want to continue our relationship it will likely need to be at a (higher price, greater volume, faster cycle time, lower cost, etc.)."

The goal is to cordially communicate that you can no longer cost-justify a lose-win customer relationship, especially when the financial health of your business is at issue. You will want to be crystal clear on intent and speak with unequivocal conviction.

WHEN FIRING FOR EMOTIONAL OR VALUES-RELATED REASONS

As furious, defensive or protective as you may feel in these more emotionally charged firing situations, your rage will simply fuel the customer's anger at being let go. Again, a rational explanation for why a continued relationship will harm your business—how harsh treatment of service reps impairs productivity, or how a difficult relationship steals time from other deserving customers—should be your modus operandi here.

If a customer firing is in defense of associates or values, it should also proclaim "Stop! We do not tolerate those actions here." The goal is to give the customer a signal that he or she is unwelcome if the unwanted behavior persists. "Ms. Jones, I must ask you to leave. The morale of our associates is critically important to their own well-being and to the well-being of our organization. While we are by no means perfect, our employees must not be repeatedly subjected to actions that demean them as people." The goal isn't to send customers on an extended guilt trip, only to clearly state the facts and why continuing the relationship isn't in the best interests of the organization.

WHEN "FIRING" A CAPTIVE CUSTOMER

So, what if your customers are your colleagues or you are a protected/regulated monopoly (utilities, government services) and have customers who are trapped and cannot leave? Obviously, you do not have the freedom to tell such a customer farewell. What you can do is be very firm and direct about the importance of your integrity, self-esteem, or values. Many customers, even those with a malicious streak, will admire someone who stands up for what is important to them. As a step short of firing, consider letting someone else in your unit work with this particular customer. Sometimes there are personality clashes, even among service providers trying to do their very best.

Firing any customer, no matter how toxic or marginally profitable, might seem heresy in today's highly competitive, digitally connected markets where companies fight tooth and nail to attract new customers. Yet courageously ending relationships with customers who continually turn the blowtorch on the front line, or who over time siphon more funds from the bottom line than they return, sends a message about what you stand for as a unit or organization.

Tool #11

For Conducting Customer Forensics

Columbo was a wildly popular television series in the 1970s. Peter Falk portrayed Lieutenant Columbo, a seemingly naïve, disorganized investigator attempting to unravel a crime. Most episodes started by showing the culprit committing the crime. The entertainment of the program came through watching Columbo meticulously solve the whodunit. His greatest tool was his ability to play dumb and thus reassure his target, who then unwittingly provided the clues that helped Columbo put the disparate pieces together.

Forensics is the examination of evidence using a broad spectrum of disciplines to arrive at a conclusion or insight. **Customer forensics** is typically used as a postmortem examination of customer information to determine the real cause for the loss of the customer. It asks us to be like Columbo. The understanding gained can point the way to improvements useful in curbing future customer churn or turnover.

One of the tools most valuable in conducting customer forensics comprises questions to ask a customer you lost (especially one you did not want to lose). Begin the conversation by letting the customer know that your goal is learning, not reclaiming the customer's allegiance. If customers smell a backhanded sales call, they will withhold the information you need.

The hardest part of a customer forensic inquiry is remaining completely non-judgmental. Demonstrate curiosity, not defensiveness. There will be times in the conversation you will want to "straighten the customer out" because of inaccuracies on which they are basing their view. Again, your goal is to learn, not to teach, correct, or fix. The more customers talk, the more they tend to talk. The more customers talk about a single subject, the deeper they will go into that subject. Most important, the more customers feel free to focus on their areas of interest or concern, the more will be revealed. The more that is revealed, the more you will learn.

Try some of these questions:

- What are your expectations of an organization in our industry? Of our organization?

- What is one aspect about our organization that you view as "very positive"?

- What organization do you consider to be the best service provider in your life? If that particular organization ran ours, what do you think they might do differently?

- If you were picking the five best service providers in your life, would our organization be among the top five? Why/why not?

- What is one aspect of our organization that you view as "needing improvement"?

- If you could be the president of our organization for one week, and your goal was to make it an organization renowned for great customer service, what would you change first? What else would you do?

- Complete this sentence: What I like least about what you do is . . .

- Complete this sentence: What I like most about what you do is . . .

- When you think about working with our organization, what are the first words that come to mind?

- Thinking about the people you deal with at our organization, what are they like? What would make them more effective? If you owned an organization in our industry, would you hire them?

- Recall a time when we left you disappointed. Briefly describe the incident. What did they do to recover, to return your feelings at least back to satisfaction? What should they have done?

- What would you like to see us do that no other organization is currently doing?

- If you were on a team to completely redesign the way organizations in our industry serve customers, what would you focus on first?

- What are the top two criteria you utilize to select an organization in our industry?

- Thinking about our organization, what words come to mind when I say:

  — Easy to deal with

  — Bureaucracy

  — A great value for the price

- — Quality

- — Personalized service

- What have we not asked that we should ask?

Tool #12

For Determining If Your Service Process Is Unwell

The Native Americans believe every creation has a soul. A tree possesses a spirit in the same way as a horse, bird or human being, which engenders a feeling of oneness with nature and a focus on conservation. Organizations that create loyal customers look at their processes in a similar way. Customer-centric organizations examine their processes to be certain that they correctly deliver the appropriate signals to customers.

A "live" perspective ensures that key service processes receive the proper care and feeding, so they don't fall into disrepair and consistently fail to deliver the kind of hassle-free, friendly service experiences that create distinction in the market. Cumbersome processes are the bane of customer loyalty.

A process might be governed by a set of procedures (fill out the application in triplicate, or listen to ten voice-response-unit options before making a choice), a collection of regulations (complete in one hour and provide a copy to security), or even certain laws (enter into the company ledger). But while the primary role of processes is to ensure that service is delivered in a consistent and efficient fashion, there is no law stating they should also make customers want to pull their hair out.

There are a number of tests for diagnosing the health of your processes. Here are seven:

1. *Are your processes designed from the customers' perspective?* The customer perspective trumps processes built for internal convenience every time.

2. *Are your processes in sync with the organization's vision?* If the service vision is about "responsiveness," then every process must be crafted to facilitate responsiveness. Processes must also always defer to the organization's core values and standards. Values and standards take precedence over processes and procedures.

3. *Do your processes facilitate great internal service, not just external service?* The existence of silos and shaky hand-offs between departments hurts process morale. Silos can be real, or just an attitude. In either case they are a barrier to great service because they prevent the smooth transition from one aspect of customer service to another (internal and external) or they create issues that impact customers between steps in a process.

4. *Are process changes driven by "economics" scrutinized for their impact on customers before an accurate return on investment can be determined?* Too often organizations evaluate the economics of process change solely on the "ROI" of their investment in the change itself, without attaching any value to the impact the change may have on customers.

5. *Are processes regularly updated to ensure they reflect customers' ever-changing expectations for service?* The ten top most important processes—those deemed to have the biggest impact on customer loyalty—must be subjected to an annual "alignment check" and tuneup. Today's expectations change at supersonic speed as wired customers are influenced by their experiences with organizations of every type and effectiveness.

6. *Are processes that cease to achieve their purpose eliminated before their continued presence fools someone into thinking they are needed, and they begin to fall under "special protection" by their custodian?* Processes that have been in place for

an extended period tend to become overly respected and can become thought of as untouchable.

7. *Are all processes employee friendly?* Research has shown that engaged and loyal employees are needed to drive the type of service that produces loyal customers.[9] Just as you would use filters to ensure processes reflect the organization's service vision, so too should you use employee engagement as a "filter" for testing a process's impact on the employees who are affected by it.

Tool #13

For Adding Decoration to the Service Experience

When you arrive at a Cracker Barrel restaurant, the first thing you notice are the scores of rocking chairs across the sprawling front porch that invite a cozy conversation. Just in case you have a bit of a wait, there are tables with large checkerboards and checkers for a quick game to help you pass the time. When you cross the threshold into the restaurant, your nose knows the scent of sassafras candy canes, your ears detect bluegrass music, and your eyes spot artifacts hanging from the ceiling as if plucked straight from an old-fashioned general store: cast iron skillets, washboards, and pitchforks. The menu reads like a gourmet "who's who" from somebody's grandmother's cupboard—chicken and dumplings, fried okra, sugar-cured ham, and apple cider. The wait staff greeting sets a new standard for a perfect Tennessee "How ya'll doin'" drawl.

What's happening in this picture? You are experiencing an enterprise magnifying the power of the five senses to augment the customer's service experience. Some organizations perform decoration with the bravado of Disney's Rain Forest Restaurant, a cacophony of sensory overload. Some are so subtle that only the customer's subconscious picks up the signal. When realtors suggest baking an apple pie before holding an open house, when cookie shops pipe their kitchen aroma onto the sidewalk, and when upscale retail stores put a pianist at a baby grand on the sales floor, all are declaring the common sense of uncommon sense appeal.

Learn from the best at sensory enhancement. Take a walk through Bellagio, the Venetian, or the MGM Grand on your next trip to Vegas. How do they blend music, mural, mystery, and magic? Log on to the websites of Omiru, Popsugar, Picnik, Howcast, or iliketotallyloveit. You'll find a treasure trove of sensory delights to adapt to your own situation.

What associations might be caused by each sense attraction you consider? Sights, sounds, and smells are all cues for customers that can surface pleasant or not-so-pleasant memories. A sign with red lettering might send a different message than the same sign in green. If it's ten degrees below zero outside, a silk kimono in the hotel guest's closet isn't nearly as sensuous as a thick terrycloth bathrobe.

When you have chosen the senses you want to appeal to, find ways to introduce them so that customers can discover them gradually. Remember that sensory enhancement must reflect proportion and balance. Christmas trees are not the same visual experience if a few flashy ornaments grab all the attention. If your customers are singing along with the music, it might be playing too loud.

Tool #14

For Designing a Survey Your Customers Will Actually Complete

Here are some design ideas:

1. Use a personal connection to alert customers that a survey is on its way and is important.

2. Ask for your customers' help in the opening communication.

3. Use a stamp for mailed surveys.

4. Keep the number of questions fewer than twelve—ten if possible!

5. Make questions sound like a conversation.

6. Surveys need to have emotional attraction. Make yours interesting and appealing.

7. Make the survey and envelope look unique and intriguing.

8. Let respondents know why you are conducting the survey and what will happen with the results.

9. Make the survey matter to them.

10. Make the survey matter, period!

One more thought: Regardless of the scientific gobbledygook you are likely to get from the folks down in market research, asking your customers to rate their service experience from "unsatisfied" to "very satisfied" is like asking them to give you no grade higher than a C!

As we earlier described, satisfied means "met my needs," was "adequate" or "sufficient." It also means "finished, done, no more for me." Look it up in the dictionary! If you asked a 10-year-old to evaluate her weekend at Disneyworld, you are not likely to hear "I was very satisfied." Service is emotional. Use the language that fits!

FlashDrive
Favorites

Favorite #1

Best Books on Understanding the Wired and Dangerous Customer

Bernoff, Josh and Ted Schadler. *Empowered: Unleash Your Employees, Energize Your Customers, and Transform Your Business.* Boston: Harvard Business Press, 2010.

Berry, Leonard L. *Discovering the Soul of Service: The Nine Drivers of Sustainable Business Success.* New York: The Free Press, 1999.

Bliss, Jeanne. *I Love You More Than My Dog: Five Decisions That Drive Extreme Customer Loyalty in Good Times and Bad.* New York: Penguin Group, 2009.

Godin, Seth. *Linchpin: Are You Indispensible?* New York: Portfolio Hardcover, 2009.

Goodman, John A. *Strategic Customer Service: Managing the Customer Experience to Increase Positive Word of Mouth, Build Loyalty, and Maximize Profits.* New York: AMACOM, 2009.

Hsieh, Tony. *Delivering Happiness: A Path to Profits, Passion, and Purpose.* New York: Business Plus, 2010.

Hunt, Tara. *The Whuffie Factor: Using the Power of Social Networking to Build Your Business.* New York: Crown Books, 2009.

Li, Charlene and Josh Bernoff. *Groundswell: Winning in a World Transformed by Social Technologies.* Boston: Harvard Business Press, 2008.

Ott, Adrian C. *The 24-Hour Customer: New Rules for Winning in a Time-Starved, Always-Connected Economy.* New York: Harper-Collins, 2010.

Scoble, Robert and Shel Israel. *Naked Conversations: How Blogs Are Changing the Way Businesses Talk with Customers.* New York: Wiley, 2006.

Scott, David M. *The New Rules of Marketing and PR: How to Use News Releases, Blogs, Podcasting, Viral Marketing, and Online Media to Reach Buyers Directly,* 2nd ed. New York: Wiley, 2010.

Smith, Shaun and Andy Milligan. *Bold: How to Be Brave in Business and Win.* London: Kogan Page, 2011.

Zemke, Ron and Tom Connellan. *E-Service: 24 Ways to Keep Your Customers—When the Competition Is Just a Click Away.* New York: AMACOM, 2001.

And, we are very proud of some we have written:

Bell, Chip R. and John R. Patterson. *Take Their Breath Away: How Imaginative Service Creates Devoted Customers.* NY: Wiley, 2009.

Bell, Chip R. and John R. Patterson. *Customer Loyalty Guaranteed: Create, Lead, and Sustain Remarkable Customer Service.* Avon, MA: Adams Business, 2007.

Bell, Chip R. and Bilijack R. Bell. *Magnetic Service: Secrets for Creating Passionately Devoted Customers.* San Francisco: Berrett-Koehler Publishers, 2004.

Bell, Chip R. *Customers as Partners: Building Relationships That Last.* San Francisco: Berrett-Koehler, 1994.

Bell, Chip R. and Ron Zemke. *Managing Knock Your Socks off Service,* 2nd ed. New York: AMACOM Books, 2007. Originally published 1992.

Favorite #2

Best Websites for Understanding the Wired and Dangerous Customer

www.amazingserviceguy.com: A free online resource to help improve customer service. Trainer and consultant Kevin Stirtz is the creator and caretaker of the site that features over 800 free articles and other resources.

www.bain.com: A large worldwide business strategy consulting firm. Their customer strategy and marketing practice has pioneered many cutting-edge advances, including the popular NetPromoter. Their site provides articles, Bain briefs, and newsletters.

www.churchofthecustomer.com: Ranked as one of the most popular business blogs in the world with more than 121,000 readers, co-authors Ben McConnell and Jackie Huba deliver unique insights on how to build word of mouth into the DNA of organizations and how to create customer evangelism strategies.

www.cmocouncil.org: The Chief Marketing Officer Council is dedicated to high-level knowledge exchange, thought leadership, and personal relationship-building among senior corporate marketing leaders. Operated by Global Fluency, it provides helpful featured reports.

www.convergys.com: One of the leading U.S. consulting firms specializing in value-added relationship management, customer management solutions, and BSS solutions offers blogs, thought leader-authored white papers, webinars, and podcasts. Convergys' sweet spot includes the use of smart technology to improve the effectiveness of call centers.

www.customerbliss.com: Home of the blog "Customer Experience Snack" written by Jeanne Bliss, bestselling author of *Chief Customer Officer* and *I Love You More Than My Dog*. Jeanne has twenty-five years as the Customer Experience Executive in five major U.S. corporations and dedicates her blog to creating clarity and an action-able path for driving the customer loyalty commitment into business operations.

www.customersrock.net: Watch out for the .net! A website created by Becky Carroll of Petra Consulting Group, a long-time customer advocate and customer conversation specialist. The site provides a constant stream of thought-provoking blogs.

www.customerservicemanager.com is an online community and e-magazine for customer service professionals. The site is chock-full of helpful news, practical reviews and insightful articles aimed at improving customer service worldwide. The current events sec-tion provides a solid means to link to best practices and resources.

www.customerthink.com: A global online community of business leaders striving to create profitable customer-centric enterprises. Each month the site reaches over 200,000 subscribers and visitors from 200 countries. Its main areas of coverage are Customer Rela-tionship Management, Customer Experience Management, and Social Business. This is a great place to learn about every facet of customer-centric business management in articles, blogs, interviews, and news.

www.ducttapemarketing.com: Written by John Jantsch, author of *Duct Tape Marketing* and *The Referral Engine,* the blog provides small-business readers with successful marketing techniques that don't require a large budget to execute. Full of tips, strategies, and tactics to help entrepreneurs expand their businesses as well as maximize the use of social media.

www.forrester.com: A global technology and market research company that provides pragmatic advice to global leaders in busi-ness and technology. Their white papers present some of the most quoted customer research findings in the world.

www.1to1media.com: Created by the independent publishing di-vision of Peppers & Rogers Group, a management consulting firm focused on customer-based strategies and underlying business ini-tiatives. Full of cutting-edge tips on treating different customers differently and better understanding the value that your customers create.

www.perfectcustomerexperience.com: Started by Dale Wolf and focused on promoting customer experience management. Features a number of prominent authors, including Jeanne Bliss and Shaun Smith, as regular contributors. Filled with great tips on delivering an outstanding customer experience. Offers a unique perspective on the customer experience in health care.

www.qualitydigest.com: A community that covers a wide range of general-interest quality topics. The Quality Insider section of the website and the *Quality Digest Magazine* (also online) often contain articles on customer service quality.

www.qualityservicemarketing.com: Website focused on helping service providers take care of the people who most impact their marketing and organizational success. QSM has developed practical tools of engagement that assist organizations in gaining employee commitment and strengthening employee-customer relationships, as well as creating and reinforcing a customer-focused service culture.

www.serviceinstitute.com: The Customer Service Institute of America manages the International Service Excellence Awards. These awards are the world's peak customer service awards with leading customer service organizations and individuals around the globe being nominated to recognize their commitment to customer service excellence. CSIA also provides ongoing professional development of customer facing and contact-center service professionals, customer service managers, and Chief Customer Officers.

www.serviceuntitled.com: A leading blog on customer service and the customer service experience. The writers behind Service Untitled focus on pragmatic and simple solutions to real customer service problems that can help set a company apart from its competition, and on how to go about implementing industry-leading customer service processes and procedures.

www.sethgodin.com: Seth Godin has written 12 bestsellers that have been translated into 33 languages. He writes about the post-industrial revolution, the way ideas spread, marketing, quitting, leadership and, most of all, changing everything. *American Way* magazine calls him "America's Greatest Marketer," and his blog is perhaps the most popular in the world written by a single individual.

www.shaunsmithco.com: Website created and managed by smith+co, a London-based consulting firm that helps organizations define and deliver a distinctive customer experience. The site provides an array of thought-provoking blogs and CEM (Customer Experience Management) tips.

www.smallbusinessadvocate.com: Website that delivers valuable original information to help small-business owners and managers have the maximum opportunity to be successful. Here you will find thousands of multi-media resources provided by hundreds of experts—the Brain Trust—including founder Jim Blasingame. Google ranks Jim as the #1 small-business expert in the world.

www.vovici.com: Leading provider of intelligent online survey management and feedback solutions. Vovici's core values are: People who rock, Need for speed, "No name" jerseys, The right stuff, and Great Neighbors.

Favorite #3

Favorite Service Quotes

"Breakthroughs come from an instinctive judgment of what customers might want if they knew to think about it."
Andrew Grove, Former CEO of Intel

"A guest sees more in an hour than the host in a year."
Polish proverb

"Customers who consider our waitresses uncivil should see the manager."
Sign in a restaurant

"Never doubt that a small group of thoughtful and committed people can change the world. Indeed, it's the only thing that ever has."
Margaret Mead

"Give all thou canst; high heaven rejects the lore of nicely-calculated less or more."
William Wordsworth

"Life isn't measured by the breaths you take but by the things that take your breath away."
George Carlin

"A complaining customer is my best friend."
Stew Leonard, Sr., CEO,
Stew Leonard's Dairy Stores

"Reserved parking for garage staff only. All others will be towed."
Sign over the best parking spaces at an upscale retail shopping center

"Consumers are statistics; customers are people."
Stanley Marcus, Founder of Neiman-Marcus

"Just because customers don't complain doesn't mean all parachutes are perfect."
Benny Hill

"Even if you could genetically engineer a six-sigma goat, if your market is a rodeo, your customers will prefer a four-sigma horse."
                    Chip Bell

"All of our Christmas trees are adjustable . . . we have a chainsaw!"
                    Steven W. Gross

"My three basic rules are these: be passionate, tell personal stories, and be real."
                    Tony Hsieh

Favorite #4

Twenty Things Today's Wired and Dangerous Customers Really Want

1. Make me smarter . . . it helps me keep up with my ever-changing world.

2. Help me do it myself . . . I enjoy feeling self-sufficient.

3. Make the response fast . . . but don't sacrifice quality—quick and rushed aren't the same.

4. Help me customize the experience . . . I want it like I want it.

5. Anchor your offering to a cause I believe in . . . good works works, and sells.

6. Entertain me . . . make the experience bright, shiny, and memorable.

7. Don't invade my privacy . . . never let me worry about whether you know too much about me.

8. Respect my time . . . make your offering super-easy to deal with.

9. Anticipate my needs . . . it tells me you really understand me.

10. Treat me with respect when things go wrong . . . not some cheap, generic atonement unmatched to the incident.

11. Never take me for granted . . . I will drop you in a heartbeat.

12. When you make a mistake, tell me the truth . . . it shows me you care.

13. Link me to a professional team . . . not a single person who may leave.

14. My time is just as important as my funds . . . maybe more.

15. Help me integrate . . . link stuff together to increase the efficiency of my life.

16. Life is complex . . . make your service simple.

17. Life is harried . . . make your service calm.

18. Life can be shallow . . . make your service have resonance and depth.

19. Life can be painful . . . make your service joyful.

20. Life can be lonely . . . make your service a valued connection and a community.

Favorite #5

Favorite Metaphor for Turning "Dangerous" Customers into Advocates

Several years ago Logan Graves posted the "50 Rules of Combat: They Never Taught You" on his website.[1] We filed the clever set of rules away but recently dusted them off for a fresh look at remarkable service. Here are a few of his rules.

1. *The easy way is always mined.*

   There is an adage that goes "only dead fish swim with the current." Great service seeks the road less traveled in the pursuit of ingenious and novel. Today's customers are bored with pretty good service.

2. *No combat-ready unit ever passed inspection; no inspection-ready unit ever passed combat.*

   Great service is scrappy and provocative. It focuses on what works, not on what's cute. The "function over form" orientation enables you to race past preoccupation with appearance to outpace those mired in convention.

3. *Your enemy is never a villain in his own eyes.*

   Great service providers are intensely competitive—with their own standards of excellence. "Beating the competition" is not their internal driver, rather it is "delivering the goods" better than their adversary. While never oblivious to where they are in their relationship with others, their energy is fueled by an internal intent to excel, not by a malevolent motivation to defeat. They focus on their vision and goals rather than on their opponent and the scoreboard.

4. *All five-second grenade fuses are three seconds.*

   Great service requires preparation, not serendipity. Dancers do rehearsal, planners create what-if scenarios, and product makers use dry runs. Granted, everything cannot be pilot tested. But remarkable service providers know that mastering the unexpected comes through forethought and study.

5. *When the pin is pulled, Mr. Grenade is NOT our friend.*

   Great service requires the courage to try new and different. And, such courage comes from a sense of accountability to those you serve. It enables you to embrace challenge as a chance to test limits and reaffirm principles.

Would your customers describe you as brave or courageous? Do you celebrate excellent efforts that fail? Are you constantly seeking a path to new experiences your customers will find memorable as well as valuable?

Favorite # 6

A Poem on Customers as Partners

Partnership . . .
>The word is spoken with such ease, and
>pictures parade before our mind's eye.
>We scan this collage in search of meaning
>in this concept deserving of softer syllables.
>We see a picture of colleagues,
>their letters speaking their story . . .
>Inc., P.A., Ltd., and associates.
>We see a picture of couples,
>their rings telling their theme . . .
>dearly beloved, oh promise me, I do.
>We see a picture of alliances,
>their photos narrating their news . . .
>CEO 1 shakes hands with CEO 2.
>But what does partnership mean?
>After the business cards are printed,
>and the wedding cake is cut,
>and the boardroom is silent . . . what's left?
>Partnership is a bond of kindred spirits
>seeking
>a setting for truth,
>a context for trust, and
>a crucible for generosity.
>Partnership is a verb disguised as a noun.

It is a force released,
"un-nouned,"
when dreams connect
and service is gracefully given.

> From *Customers as Partners: Building Relationships That Last,* by Chip R. Bell (San Francisco: Berrett-Koehler Publishers, 1994). Used by permission.

Notes

Part One: The Situation
Welcome to Turbulent Times!

1. Matt Richtel, "Attached to Technology and Paying a Price," www.nytimes. com, June 6, 2010.

2. Society for New Communications Research, "New Study Indicates Consumers Use Social Media to Share Customer Care Experiences and Research Companies' Customer Service Reputations," April 22, 2008.

3. "United Airlines and Consumer Generated Turbulence," www.nielsen.com/ blogs, July 16, 2009.

4. Courtesy of Convergys 2010 Customer Scorecard Research, www.convergys. com/research. Used with permission.

5. Ibid.

6. "Forrester Forecast: Online Retail Sales Will Grow to \$250B by 2014," by Erick Schonfeld, March 8, 2010, www.techcrunch.com.

7. See American Express, "Americans Will Spend 9% More with Companies That Provide Excellent Service," July 7, 2010, http://about.americanexpress. com/news/pr/2010/barometer.aspx (Viewed October 29, 2010)

8. Lora Kolodny, "Study: 82% Of U.S. Consumers Bail On Brands After Bad Customer Service," www.techcrunch.com, October 13, 2010.

Chapter 1 How the Service Covenant Became Corrupted

1. Karl Albrecht and Ron Zemke, *Service America in the New Economy* (New York: McGraw-Hill, 2002), 56–57.

2. Some content in this section was adapted from "Serving the Post-Recession Customer," by Chip R. Bell, *MWorld*, Fall 2010, 27–29.

3. Reported in *I Live in the Future and Here's How it Works*, by Nick Bilton (New York: Crown Business, 2010), 109.

4. George Santayana, *The Life of Reason*, Vol. 1, 1905.

5. "Survey: Outsourcing Call Centers Is Bad for the Bottom Line," Inside Quality Insider, www.qualitydigest.com, August 30, 2010.

6. Ben Mutzabaugh, "Weary of Online Booking, Clients Return to Travel Agents," *USAToday*, November 16, 2010, 1.

7. Voltaire, *La Begueule* (1772).

8. Voltaire, *Philosophical Dictionary* (1764).

Chapter 2 Picky: Why Today's Customers Are Finicky

1. Courtesy of Convergys 2010 Customer Scorecard Research, www.convergys.com/research. Used with permission.

2. Ibid.

3. Ibid.

4. Accenture. Outlook. Point of View January 2008. http://www.accenture.com/Global/Research and Insights/Outlook (accessed October 19, 2010).

5. Society for New Communications Research. Exploring the Link Between Customer Care and Brand Reputation in the Age of Social Media, April, 22, 2008, http://sncr.org/2008/04/22/ (accessed October 19, 2010).

6. Josh Bernoff and Ted Schadler, "Introducing Peer Influence Analysis: 500 billion peer impressions per year," April 20, 2010, http://forrester.typepad.com/groundswell/2010/04/ (accessed October 8, 2010).

7. Ginger Conlon, "Does Customer Experience Really Matter?" One-to-One Media.com blog, Sept. 27, 2010 at http://www.1to1media.com/weblog/2010/09/ (accessed October 19, 2010).

8. "Customer Experience Impact: North America 2010," conducted by Harris Interactive and sponsored by RightNow Technologies, www.rightnow.com.

9. Courtesy of Convergys 2010 Customer Scorecard Research, www.convergys.com/research. Used with permission.

Chapter 3 Fickle: Why Today's Customers Are Capricious

1. Accenture Outlook, Point of View, February 2010, http://www.accenture
   .com/Global/Research_and_Insights/Outlook/POV/Feb2010/customerloyalty.
   htm.

2. Courtesy of Convergys 2010 Customer Scorecard Research, www.convergys.
   com/research. Used with permission.

3. Accenture Outlook, Point of View, February 2010, http://www.accenture
   .com/Global/Research_and_Insights/Outlook/POV/Feb2010/customerloyalty.
   htm.

4. Accenture Institute for High Performance, Business Research Note, March
   2008, http://www.accenture.com/Global/Research_and_Insights/Institute-
   For-High-Performance/By_Subject/Marketing/ReducingDefection.htm.

5. Courtesy of Convergys 2010 Customer Scorecard Research, www.convergys.
   com/research. Used with permission.

6. Ibid.

7. Ibid.

8. Steve Martin, "An Hour with Steve Martin," interview on *The Char-
   lie Rose Show,* December 12, 2007, http://www.charlierose.com/view/
   interview/8831(accessed October 28, 2010).

9. Marcel Fenez and Marieke van der Donk, "Multiple Business Models: Outlook for Newspapers in the Digital Age," PricewaterhouseCoopers white,
   2009, 33.

Chapter 4 Vocal: Why Today's Customers Are Noisy

1. 2005 Respond Study, reported at "Capturing Customer Feedback," Unica,
   The Marketers Consortium, http://unicashare.typepad.com/share/2006/10/
   capturing_custo.html (accessed December 8, 2010).

2. Courtesy of Convergys 2010 Customer Scorecard Research, www.convergys.
   com/research. Used with permission.

3. John Blasberg, Vijay Vishwanath, and James Allen, "Tools for Converting
   Consumers into Advocates," *Strategy and Leadership,* March 1, 2008.

4. H.B. Beckman and R.M. Frankel, "The effect of physician behavior on the
   collection of data," *Annals of Internal Medicine* 1984: 101:692–6.

5. Pete Blackshaw, *Satisfied Customers Tell Three Friends, Angry Customers Tell
   3000*: Running a Business in Today's Consumer-Driven World (New York:
   Doubleday, 2008), 11.

6. Courtesy of Convergys 2010 Customer Scorecard Research, www.convergys. com/research. Used with permission.

7. Ibid.

8. "Think Customers," The 1 to 1 Blog, 10/21/2010, http://www.1to1media. com/weblog/.

9. Courtesy of Convergys 2010 Customer Scorecard Research, www.convergys. com/research. Used with permission.

10. *Harris Interactive, Customer Experience Impact Report,* reported in TechCrunch. com blog, "82% of Customers Bail on Brands after Bad Service," by Lora Kolodny, October 13, 2010.

11. Courtesy of Convergys 2010 Customer Scorecard Research, www.convergys. com/research. Used with permission.

12. http://www.youtube.com/watch?v=xmpDSBAh6RY (accessed October 8, 2010).

13. The blog by Ben Popken on "The Consumerist" website appeared on July 18, 2006. See http://consumerist.com/2006/07/aol-retention-manual-revealed. html (accessed December 8, 2010).

14. Ibid.

15. Sue Shellenbarger, "Beyond Facebook: The Benefits of Deeper Friendships," *Wall Street Journal,* November 10, 2010, D3.

16. For more on the admiral's story, see James Stockdale, *A Vietnam Experience: Ten Years of Reflection* (Palo Alto: Board of Trustees of the Leland Stanford Junior University, 1984).

17. Parmy Olson, "A Twitterati Calls Out Whirlpool," www.forbes.com, September 2, 2009.

18. Society for New Communications Research, "Exploring the Link Between Customer Care and Brand Reputation in the Age of Social Media," April, 22, 2008, http://sncr.org/2008/04/22/new-study-indicates-consumers-use-social-media-to-share-customer-care-experiences-and-research-companies%E2%80%99-customer-service-reputations/.

19. Christine Mosnik, "Introverts, Extroverts and Communication," www. suite101.com, March 2, 2010.

20. Amanda Kooser, "New Mexico Tea Company: How Loyal Customers Saved a Business," AOL Small Business Blog September 12, 2010.

http://smallbusiness.aol.com/2010/09/12/new-mexico-tea-company-how-loyal-customers-saved-a-business/ (accessed October 19, 2010).

Chapter 5 Vain: Why Today's Customers Are Self-Centered

1. Zachary Wilson, "Coca-Cola's 100-Flavor Interactive Freestyle Soda Fountain in Action," www.fastcompany.com, July 21, 2009.

2. Rimma Katz, "eBay, Amazon Dominate 70 Percent of Mobile Commerce Market: Panelist," Mobile Commerce Daily, March 5, 2010, www.mobilecommercedaily.com.

3. Quote by John Donahoe from the *International Herald Tribune,* July 17, 2008, reported on www.genuineseller.com, "John Donahoe Quotes—A Year in Review."

4. Gwendolyn Bounds, "The Rise of Holiday Me-tailers," *Wall Street Journal,* December 8, 2010, p D1.

5. Justina Janusz, "Mini Says a 'High-Tech Hello' to Its Drivers," February 27, 2007, www.forbesautos.com.

6. Ben McConnell, "Extending the personal touch," www.churchofthecustomer.com, September 30, 2006.

7. "An 'eHarmony' of call centers emerges: New method matches each caller with best representative." By Mary Welch, Atlanta Journal-Constitution, January 2, 2011, D1.

8. Ibid.

9. *Marketing Customer Relationships: A Strategic Framework* by Don Peppers and Martha Rogers (New York: Wiley, 2011), 287.

10. O.J. Postma and M. Brokke, "Personalization in practice: The proven effects of personalization," *Journal of Database Management* 9(2), 2002, 137–42.

11. Asim Ansari and Carl F. Mela, "E-Customization," *Journal of Marketing Research* 40 (2), 131–45.

12. Edward C. Malthouse and Ralf Elsner, "Customization with Cross-Basis Sub-Segmentation," *Database Marketing and Customer Strategy Management* 14(1), 2006, 40–50.

Part Two: The Resolution
Manifesto: The Wired and Dangerous Link

1. "A Narrative History of Sears," www.searsarchives.com.

2. Letty Cottin Pogrebin, "What the Pill Did," www.cnn.com, May 6, 2010.

3. Blackshaw, Pete, *Satisfied Customers Tell Three Friends, Angry Customers Tell 3,000: Running a Business in Today's Consumer-Driven World* (New York: Doubleday, 2008), 3.

4. Ibid.

5. Tara Hunt, *The Whuffie Factor: Using the Power of Social Networking to Build Your Business* (New York: Crown Business, 2009), 4.

6. "From Major to Minor," The Economist, January 15, 2008 and quoted in Hunt, *The Whuffie Factor*, p. 12.

7. Courtesy of Convergys 2010 Customer Scorecard Research, www.convergys.com/research. Used with permission.

8. Kim Williams, "Dell Hell: The Impact of Social Media on Corporate Communication," https://learningspaces.njit.edu/elliot/content/dell-hell-impact-social-media-corporate-communication.

9. The American Customer Satisfaction Index reports scores on a 0–100 scale at the national level and produces indexes for 10 economic sectors, 43 industries (including e-commerce and e-business), and more than 200 companies and federal or local government agencies. The ACSI is managed by the University of Michigan Ross School of Business, www.theacsi.org.

10. Leanne Hoagland-Smith, "Your Company's Bottom Line Is Tied to Customer Satisfaction,"www.customerservicemanager.com, http://customerservicemanager.com/how-your-companys-bottom-line-is-tied-to-customer-satisfaction.htm (accessed December 12, 2010).

Chapter 6 How the Service Covenant Can Be Rebalanced

1. See, for example, http://www.answers.com/topic/customer-service. Originally quoted in Efraim Turban, *Electronic Commerce: A Managerial Perspective* (Upper Saddle River, NJ: Prentice Hall, 2002).

2. *National Treasure*. Jerry Bruckheimer, producer. Walt Disney Pictures, 2004.

Chapter 7 Grounding: How to Balance Yourself for Partnership

1. Some of this content is adapted from *Customer Loyalty Guaranteed* by Chip R. Bell and John R. Patterson (Avon, MA: Adams Business, 2007).

Chapter 8 Connection: How to Help Customers Feel Like Partners

1. See, for example, http://images.businessweek.com/ss/10/02/0218_customer_service_champs/1.htm.
2. Courtesy of Convergys 2010 Customer Scorecard Research, www.convergys.com/research. Used with permission.
3. Ibid.

Chapter 9 Bad Connections: How to Turn Angry Customers into Partners

1. Valarie A. Zeithaml, A. Parasuraman, and Leonard Berry, *Delivering Quality Service: Balancing Customer Perceptions and Expectations* (New York: Free Press, 1990), 126.
2. Ron Zemke and Chip R. Bell, *Knock Your Socks Off Service Recovery* (New York: AMACOM Books, 2000), 47.
3. Jeffrey Henning, "The Service Recovery Paradox: No Excuse for Bad Service." www.vovici.com July 13, 2010. Based on Stefan Michel and Matthew L. Meuter (2008), "The Service Recovery Paradox: True But Overrated?" International *Journal of Service Industry Management* 19(4).

Chapter 10 Wireless Connections: How to Partner with Customers via the Internet

1. Albert Mehrabian, *Silent Messages: Implicit Communication of Emotions and Attitudes* (Belmont, CA: Wadsworth, 1981). Currently distributed by Albert Mehrabian, email: am@kaaj.com.
2. Ibid.
3. Log on to www.davecarrollmusic.com for a listen as well as the detailed version of his side of the story.
4. Courtesy of Convergsys 2010 Customer Scorecard Research. www.convergsys.com/research. Used with permission.
5. Ibid.
6. Ibid.
7. Chris Walters, "Dave Carroll Says No to Guitar Hush Money from United," www.theconsumerist.com, July 10, 2009.

8. Robert Spector, *Anytime, Anywhere: How the Best Bricks-and-Clicks Businesses Deliver Seamless Service to Their Customers* (New York: Perseus Publishing, 2002), 60.

9. Lisa Arthur, "Have No Fear, Let Customers Control Your Brand," Think Customers: The 1to1 Blog, September 12, 2010, http://www.1to1media.com/weblog/2010/09/guest_blogger_lisa_arthur_have.html (accessed October 11, 2010).

10. Mila d'Antonio, "Mountain Dew Hands Over Its Brand to Fans," 1 to 1 Magazine, September 2010, http://www.1to1media.com/View.aspx?docid=32519. See also www.dewmocracymediahub.com

11. Lisa Arthur, op. cit.

12. Ellen Davis, "eBay CEO Discusses Mobile, Customer Feedback and Embracing Competition," www.shop.org, September, 23, 2009.

13. See http://www.blogs.marriott.com/.

14. Dan Greenfield, "United Airlines Online Public Response to Dave Carroll," www.socialmediatoday.com, July 13, 2009, http://socialmediatoday.com/SMC/109126 (accessed October 11, 2010).

15. See www.taylorguitars.com.

16. Jon Swartz, "Social Media Like Twitter Change Customer Service," *USA Today*, November 11, 2009.

17. Tina Waters, SVP Human Performance-NCO, Comcast, correspondence with authors, September 22, 2010.

Chapter 11 Congruence: How to Get the Service Setting in Balance

1. Christopher Meyer and Andre Schwager, "Understanding Customer Experience," *Harvard Business Review*, February 2007, http://hbr.org/2007/02/understanding-customer-experience/ar/1 (accessed October 13, 2010).

2. The Miller Brothers example here is adapted from a similar one in our book *Take Their Breath Away: How Imaginative Service Creates Devoted Customers* (New York: Wiley, 2009).

3. Richard Bandler and John Grinder, *The Structure of Magic, Vol. I: A Book about Language and Therapy* (Palo Alto, CA: Science and Behavior Books, 1975).

4. Seth Godin, "Don't Forget About Color," August 30, 2010, http://sethgodin.typepad.com/seths_blog/2010/08/index.html (accessed October 13, 2010). Also see www.sethgodin.com.

5. "Customer Service Goes Holographic," www.feedlbitz.com, February 1, 2011, p.1.

6. Valarie A. Zeithaml, A. Parasuraman and Leonard Berry, *Delivering Quality Service: Balancing Customer Perceptions and Expectations* (New York: The Free Press, 1990), 25.

7. "Yakety Yak," words and music by Jerry Lieber and Mike Stoller, Copyright ©1958 Sony/ATV Music Publishing LLC, Copyright renewed, All Rights Administered by Sony/ATV Music Publishing LLC, 8 Music Square West, Nashville, TN 37203, International Copyright Secured, All Rights Reserved, Reprinted by permission of Hal Leonard Corporation.

8. Courtesy of Convergys 2010 Customer Scorecard Research. www.convergys.com/research. Used with permission.

Chapter 12 Acumen: How to Keep the Customer Relationship in Balance

1. Chris Snyder, "Amazon 'Glitch' Delists Gay-Themed Books, Interwebs Cry Foul," *Wired Epicenter*, April 13, 2009, http://www.wired.com/epicenter/2009/04/amazon-sales-ra/#ixzz136qptook (accessed October 13, 2010).

2. Ted Levitt, "After the Sale Is Over," *Harvard Business Review* 61(5), (September-October 1983), 88–94.

3. Tony Hsieh, *Delivering Happiness: A Path to Profits, Passion, and Purpose* (New York: Business Plus, 2010), 143.

4. William C. Taylor, "Get Out of That Rut and into the Shower," *New York Times,* August 13, 2006.

5. Outlook Point of View, February 2010, 1, http://www.accenture.com/Global/Research_and_Insights/Outlook/POV/Feb2010/customerloyalty.htm.

6. Stephen R. Covey, *The Seven Habits of Highly Effective People* (New York: Simon & Schuster, 1989), 287.

Flash Drive
Tools

1. Example adapted from a similar one in *Service Magic: How to Amaze Your Customers* by Ron Zemke and Chip R. Bell (Chicago: Dearborn Trade, 2003).

2. Bill Marriott endorsement of *Dance Lessons: Six Steps to Great Partnerships*

in Business and Life, by Chip Bell and Heather Shea (San Francisco: Berrett-Koehler, 1998).

3. Peter Block. *Stewardship: Choosing Service over Self-Interest* (San Francisco: Berrett-Koehler, 1993), 29.

4. "Texas" Bix Bender, *Don't Squat With Yer Spurs On! A Cowboy's Guide to Life* (Layton, UT: Gibbs Smith, 1992), 46.

5. Quote by Enrique Esparza, an eyewitness to the siege of the Alamo, in Randell Jones, *In the Footsteps of Davy Crockett* (Winston-Salem, NC: John F. Blair, Publisher, 2006), 230.

6. John Bernoff and Ted Schadler, *Empowered: Unleash Your Employees, Energize Your Customers, and Transform Your Business* (Boston: Harvard Business Press, 2010), 7.

7. Leonard L. Berry. *Discovering the Soul of Service* (New York: The Free Press, 1999), 233.

8. The quotation from William James comes from *The Principles of Psychology Vol. 1,* written in 1890. A 2007 paperback reprint edition was published by Cosimo (New York); see www.cosimo.com.

Flash Drive
Favorites

1. See http://www.intercom.net/user/logan1/rules.htm.

Bibliography

Albrecht, Karl and Ron Zemke. *Service America in the New Economy.* New York: McGraw-Hill, 2002.

Barlow, Janelle and Paul Stewart. *Branded Customer Service.* San Francisco, Berrett-Koehler, 2004.

Bell, Chip R. *Customers as Partners: Building Relationships That Last.* San Francisco: Berrett-Koehler, 1994.

Bell, Chip R. and Bilijack R. Bell. *Magnetic Service: Secrets for Creating Passionately Devoted Customers.* San Francisco: Berrett-Koehler, 2004.

Bell, Chip R. and John R. Patterson. *Customer Loyalty Guaranteed: Creating, Leading, and Sustaining Remarkable Customer Service.* Avon, MA: Adams Business, 2007.

Bell, Chip R. and John R. Patterson. *Take Their Breath Away: How Imaginative Service Creates Devoted Customers.* NY: Wiley, 2009.

Bell, Chip R. and Heather Shea. *Dance Lessons: Six Steps to Great Partnerships in Business and Life.* San Francisco: Berrett-Koehler, 1998.

Bell, Chip R. and Ron Zemke. *Managing Knock Your Socks Off Service.* New York: AMACOM Books, 1992. Second edition, 2007.

Bender, "Texas" Bix. *Don't Squat With Yer Spurs On! A Cowboy's Guide to Life.* Layton, UT: Gibbs Smith, 1992.

Bernoff, Josh and Ted Schadler. *Empowered.* Boston: Harvard Business Press, 2010.

Berry, Leonard L. *Discovering the Soul of Service.* New York: The Free Press, 1999.

Bilton, Nick. *I Live in the Future & Here's How it Works.* NY: Crown Books, 2010.

Blackshaw, Pete. *Satisfied Customers Tell Three Friends, Angry Customers Tell 3,000: Running a Business in Today's Consumer-Driven World.* New York: Doubleday Business, 2008.

Gansky, Lisa. *The Mesh.* New York: Penguin Group, 2010.

Godin, Seth. *Purple Cow: Transform Your Business by Becoming Remarkable.* New York: Penguin Books, 2003.

Godin, Seth. *The Big Moo: Stop Trying to Be Perfect and Start Being Remarkable.* New York: Penguin Books, 2005.

Godin, Seth. *Free Prize Inside! The Next BIG Marketing Idea.* New York: Penguin Books, 2004.

Griffin, Jill and Michael Lowenstein. *Customer Winback.* San Francisco: Jossey-Bass, 2001.

Hsieh, Tony. *Delivering Happiness.* New York: Business Plus, 2010.

Hunt, Tara. *The Whuffie Factor.* New York: Crown Books, 2009.

Kabani, Shama Hyder. *The Zen of Social Media Marketing.* Dallas: Benbella Books, 2010.

Keiningham, Timothy and Terry Vavra. *The Customer Delight Principle.* New York: McGraw-Hill, 2001.

Li, Charlene and Josh Bernoff. *Marketing in the Groundswell.* Boston: Harvard Business Press, 2009.

Marriott, J. Willard and Kathi Ann Brown. *The Spirit to Serve: Marriott's Way.* New York: HarperCollins, 1997.

Newell, Frederick. *Loyalty.com.* New York: McGraw-Hill, 2005.

Ott, Adrain C. *The 24-Hour Customer.* New York: Harper, 2010.

Peppers, Don and Martha Rogers. *Return on Customer.* New York, Doubleday, 2005.

Pine, Joseph and James Gilmore. *Authenticity: What Consumers Really Want.* Boston: Harvard Business School Press, 2007.

Price, Bill and David Jaffe. *The Best Service Is No Service.* San Francisco: Jossey-Bass, 2008.

Reichheld, Frederick. *Loyalty Rules.* Boston: Harvard Business School Press, 2001.

Rosen, Emanuel. *The Anatomy of Buzz.* New York: Doubleday, 2000.

Scoble, Robert and Shel Israel. *Naked Conversations.* New York: Wiley, 2009.

Scott, David M. *The New Rules of Marketing and PR.* New York: Wiley, 2010.

Zemke, Ron and Chip R. Bell. *Knock Your Socks Off Service Recovery.* New York: AMACOM Books, 2000.

Zemke, Ron and Chip R. Bell. *Service Magic: How to Amaze Your Customers.* Chicago: Dearborn Trade Publishing, 2003.

Zemke, Ron and Tom Connellan. *E-Service: 24 Ways to Keep Your Customer When the Competition is Just a Click Away.* New York: AMACOM, 2001.

Thanks

Tony D'Amelio and Harry Rhoads of the Washington Speakers Bureau; Sherri Schaefer of Southern California Edison; Katy Wild and Jeri Mueller of Freeman Company; John Longstreet of Quaker Steak and Lube; Carl Sewell, Allison Cohen, and Dawn Betrus of Sewell Automotive; Linda Dirksmeyer of Aurora Health; Tina Haddad of the City of Santa Clarita, California; Ted Dwyer, Andy, Brian, and Rick DiSabatino of EDiS Corporation; Greg Miller and Robby Miller of Miller Brothers; Nabil Moubayed of Hotel Monaco Chicago; Lorena B. Harris and Jeremy Fishel of Convergys; The late Ron Zemke; Steven S. Little; Carol Roth; Penni Conner of NStar; Sara Sefcovic of Sloane & Company; Paul Cardis of Avid Ratings; Tom Morris; Dave Stauffer; Tammy Richards-LeSure of Richards Public Relations; Nettie Hartsock, Internet Publicist; Dick Leatherman; Tom Berger of the CBC Group of Merrill Lynch; Louis Delarnoux; Pat Stocker of the University of Maryland; Jim Kouzes; Christine Churchill of The Service Institute; Chris Jackson of Allstate; Diane Barton and Mike Lang of Manheim;Tom Connellan of The Connellan Group; Meghan Flynn of Stew Leonard's Dairy Store; Lisa McLeod; Janelle Barlow of TACK-USA; Dave Harris and Ted Selogie of the Oakbrook Marriott; Jack Covert of 800CEORead.com; Jason Tebeau of Savi Baby; Kitty Scott of Children's Memorial Hospital in Boston; Carolyn Castel of CVS/pharmacy; Kim Beach of Kindred Health Care; Lee Olivier and Johnny Magwood of Northeast Utilities; Jill Applegate of Performance Research Associates; and Susan Oldham, Sandra Tacuri, Fran Sims, Mike Horn, Mary Johnson, Lindsay Willis, Catherine Glawson, Jane Goldner, and Mari Pat Varga of The Chip Bell Group.

And a Special Thanks

This book has had a special cast of helpers. Leslie Stephen, our world-class editor and long-term friend, was there, as always, with her special brand of vernacular wisdom. She consistently amazed us with her capacity to quickly and skillfully make our babble sound brilliant. Neal Maillet, our Berrett-Koehler editor, was our guide, coach and inspirational leader. All the other great folks at Berrett-Koehler, especially Stephen Piersanti, Jeevan Sivasubramaniam, Dianne Plattner, Mike Crowley, David Marshall, our book designer, Adriane Bosworth, and our book producer, Detta Penna. Finally, we give a special thanks to our life partners, Nancy Rainey Bell and Katie Bunch Patterson, for their unconditional love, unrelenting patience, and ingenious inspiration. Very late at night and too early in the morning when we were our most "wired and dangerous," they never ceased their unending support. To all of you, our heartfelt thanks.

Index

About the Authors

Chip R. Bell is a senior partner with The Chip Bell Group and manages their offices near Atlanta and Dallas. Prior to starting CBG in 1980, he was Director of Management and Organization Development for NCNB (now Bank of America). Dr. Bell holds graduate degrees from Vanderbilt University and the George Washington University. He was a highly decorated infantry unit commander in Vietnam with the elite 82nd Airborne. Chip is the author or co-author of several bestselling books including *Take Their Breath Away, Customer Loyalty Guaranteed, Magnetic Service, Service Magic, Customers as Partners,* and *Managing Knock Your Socks Off Service.* He has appeared on CNBC, CNN, ABC, Fox Business Network, and Bloomberg TV, and his work has been featured in the *Wall Street Journal, Fortune, USA Today, Fast Company,* and *Business Week.* A renowned keynote speaker, Chip has served as consultant or trainer to such organizations as GE, Microsoft, CVS/pharmacy, Cadillac, Marriott, Universal Orlando, Ritz-Carlton Hotels, Harley-Davidson, Pfizer, Sears, Duke Energy, Lockheed-Martin, and Allstate.

John R. Patterson is President of the CBG affiliate, Progressive Insights, Inc., headquartered in Atlanta, Georgia, and holds a graduate degree in business from the Darden School at the University of Virginia. He is the co-author of *Take Their Breath Away: How Imaginative Service Creates Devoted Customers* and *Customer Loyalty Guaranteed: Create, Lead, and Sustain Remarkable Customer Service.* John is a sought-after speaker, and has appeared on  ABC and the Fox Business Network. His articles have appeared in numerous professional journals, including *Leadership Esxellence* and *Customer Relationship Management.* He has over twenty years of executive leadership experience in the hospitality, real estate, and financial services industries. Prior to founding Progressive Insights in 2001, his work experience included senior leadership positions with Trammell Crow Residential, NationsBank (now Bank of America), and Guest Quarters Hotels. His consulting practice helps organizations worldwide consistently deliver great customer service experiences. John's clients include McDonald's, Allstate Insurance, Texas Instruments, Cox Enterprises, SEPTA, Freeman, Northeast Utilities, Banco Popular, EDiS Company, Kaiser Permanente, Pegasus Solutions, Banco Continental de Panama, Manheim, and The College Board.

The CHIP BELL Group is a confederation of highly experienced consultants who passionately pursue one core vision—to help clients become famous for the kind of service experiences that result in devoted customers. All members of this long-term alliance are independent consultants with their own consulting practices. They periodically work together as a high-performance team on selected consulting projects. All share key values: making cutting-edge contributions both to the profession and to their clients; practicing the world-class service they encourage their clients to emulate; and, working to leave their clients with the capacity and competence to be more successful. CBG also produces training and delivers programs for all levels of the organization from frontline employees to executive leadership. Visit their website at www.wiredanddangerous.com for additional information about consulting, keynotes, and training.

Chip R. Bell
214/522-5777
chip@chipbell.com
twitter. chiprbell

John R. Patterson
770/329-1459
john@johnrpatterson.com
twitter: johnrpatt

Blog: http://www.wiredanddangerous.wordpress.com/

Chip R. Bell and Bilijack R. Bell

Magnetic Service
Secrets for Creating Passionately Devoted Customers

Do you long to build a cult-like following for your business? Would you like to have customers who don't just recommend you but assertively insist that their friends do business with you? Discover the seven "magnetic service" secrets that have created devoted fans for brands such as Starbucks, Harley-Davidson, and the Ritz-Carlton.

Paperback, 192 pages, ISBN 978-1-57675-375-0
PDF ebook, ISBN 978-1-60509-64

Chip R. Bell

Managers as Mentors
Building Partnerships for Learning, Second Edition

Chip Bell shows managers how to help associates grow and adapt in today's tumultuous organizations. Through his SAGE approach—surrendering, accepting, gifting, and extending—he helps managers establish trust; create a safe haven for risk taking; provide advice, focus, and feedback; and ensure the transfer of learning. This new edition features four chapters "for the protégé."

Paperback, 216 pages, ISBN 978-1-57675-142-8
PDF ebook, ISBN 978-1-60994-178-9

BK® Berrett–Koehler Publishers, Inc.
San Francisco, *www.bkconnection.com*   **800.929.2929**

Chip R. Bell and Heather Shea

Dance Lessons
Six Steps to Great Partnerships in Business and Life

This comprehensive guide to building partnerships with passion, quality, heart, and soul features exciting tools for selecting the right form of partnership, smart ways to accurately pick good partners, effective methods for dealing with difficult partners and partnerships, vital cues that tell you when a partnership is ready to end, helpful tips on how to end it, and more!

Hardcover, 240 pages, ISBN 978-1-57675-043-8
PDF ebook, ISBN 978-1-60994-150-5

Chip R. Bell

Customers as Partners
Building Relationships That Last

Customers as Partners examines the qualities that form the core of all lasting relationships and describes a way of business where personal interactions, not simply sales, take center stage. When you put the relationship first, customers and clients will respond in kind and will feel they have a personal stake in your success.

Hardcover, 235 pages, ISBN 978-1-881052-54-8
PDF ebook, ISBN 978-1-60509-644-5

BK Berrett–Koehler Publishers, Inc.
San Francisco, *www.bkconnection.com*   **800.929.2929**

Berrett–Koehler
Publishers

Berrett-Koehler is an independent publisher dedicated to an ambitious mission: *Creating a World That Works for All.*

We believe that to truly create a better world, action is needed at all levels—individual, organizational, and societal. At the individual level, our publications help people align their lives with their values and with their aspirations for a better world. At the organizational level, our publications promote progressive leadership and management practices, socially responsible approaches to business, and humane and effective organizations. At the societal level, our publications advance social and economic justice, shared prosperity, sustainability, and new solutions to national and global issues.

A major theme of our publications is "Opening Up New Space." Berrett-Koehler titles challenge conventional thinking, introduce new ideas, and foster positive change. Their common quest is changing the underlying beliefs, mindsets, institutions, and structures that keep generating the same cycles of problems, no matter who our leaders are or what improvement programs we adopt.

We strive to practice what we preach—to operate our publishing company in line with the ideas in our books. At the core of our approach is stewardship, which we define as a deep sense of responsibility to administer the company for the benefit of all of our "stakeholder" groups: authors, customers, employees, investors, service providers, and the communities and environment around us.

We are grateful to the thousands of readers, authors, and other friends of the company who consider themselves to be part of the "BK Community." We hope that you, too, will join us in our mission.

A BK Business Book

This book is part of our BK Business series. BK Business titles pioneer new and progressive leadership and management practices in all types of public, private, and nonprofit organizations. They promote socially responsible approaches to business, innovative organizational change methods, and more humane and effective organizations.

Berrett–Koehler
Publishers

A community dedicated to creating
a world that works for all

Vis

Rea   ad
our   s, find
out   es of
boo

Sub

Be t   fers,
exclusive a   e list
for c

Get

Berr   lers
of te   9 or
emai

Join

BKco
arour   rld
that   own
profil   ups,
post   for
upcor   e join
the c

DATE DUE

Mixed Sources
Product group from well-managed
forests and recycled wood or fiber
www.fsc.org Cert no. SW-COC-003925
© 1996 Forest Stewardship Council
FSC